JEREMIAH
BIBLE STUDY

COLOSSIANS & PHILEMON

THE LORDSHIP OF JESUS

DR. DAVID JEREMIAH

Prepared by Peachtree Publishing Services

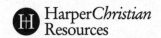

HarperChristian
Resources

COLOSSIANS & PHILEMON
JEREMIAH BIBLE STUDY SERIES

Requests for information should be addressed to:
HarperChristian Resources, 3900 Sparks Dr. SE, Grand Rapids, Michigan 49546

ISBN 978-0-310-09172-1 (softcover)
ISBN 978-0-310-09173-8 (ebook)

Produced with assistance of Peachtree Publishing Service (www.PeachtreePublishingServices.com). Project staff include Christopher D. Hudson and Randy Southern.

All Scripture quotations are taken from The Holy Bible, New King James Version. Copyright © 1979, 1980, 1982 by Thomas Nelson. All rights reserved.

Thomas Nelson titles may be purchased in bulk for educational, business, fundraising, or sales promotional use. For information, please e-mail SpecialMarkets@ThomasNelson.com.

First Printing January 2021 / Printed in the United States of America

CONTENTS

INTRODUCTION TO

The Letters of Colossians and Philemon

"We . . . do not cease to pray for you, and to ask that you may be filled with the knowledge of His will in all wisdom and spiritual understanding; that you may walk worthy of the Lord, fully pleasing Him, being fruitful in every good work and increasing in the knowledge of God; strengthened with all might, according to His glorious power, for all patience and longsuffering with joy" *(Colossians 1:9–11).* The apostle Paul wrote to the Christians in the city of Colossae to instruct and encourage them in their Christian faith. In the process, he painted one of the most vivid portraits of Jesus in all of Scripture to help the believers—and us today—understand that Christ is superior to any belief system that any false teacher tries to promote.

Paul had never been to the city of Colossae. Everything he knew about the believers in the city came from a man named Epaphras, who had likely received the message of the gospel from Paul in Ephesus. Filled with evangelistic zeal, Epaphras had returned to his hometown of Colossae to plant a church . . . and then false teachers had arrived. These were Jewish Christians who promoted a hybrid form of Christianity that included legalistic Judaism, asceticism, and worship of angels. These false teachers were also implying that Jesus and His death and resurrection were not sufficient for life and salvation.

One of the men who delivered Paul's letter to Colossae was Onesimus, a runaway slave who had become Paul's valued coworker. Onesimus's owner, Philemon, was evidently a leader in the church at Colossae. So Paul penned a personal letter to him, asking Philemon to show mercy to Onesimus, who was now also a Christian.

COLOSSIANS

Author and Date

The author of this letter identifies himself as Paul (see Colossians 1:1; 1:23; 4:18), and his opening words indicate that he was collaborating on the writing with his associate Timothy (see 1:1, 23; 4:18). He closes with a handwritten greeting (see 4:7–18), which is typical of Paul's style in his other letters. While recent scholarship has called Paul's authorship into question, early church leaders such as Irenaeus (c. AD 185) viewed the letter as genuine, and there is no textual evidence that it ever circulated under the name of any other person. The parallels between Colossians and Ephesians suggest that both letters were written by the same author at the same time and place. It is likely that Paul wrote the letter during his arrest in Rome, c. AD 60.

Background and Setting

Paul was not directly responsible for establishing the church in Colossae. Instead, Epaphras, a close associate and fellow worker, brought the gospel to the city sometime around AD 55, and he likely also founded the church at that time (see 1:7). Paul had evidently learned through Epaphras that false teachers had arrived in the city and were promoting a gospel (known only as the "Colossian heresy") that was contrary to the one that he proclaimed. Paul recognized these teachers would not stop with the Colossian church but would continue to spread their hybrid beliefs throughout Asia Minor, so he composed this forceful reminder that Christ alone finished the work of salvation—and that He alone is Lord. Many scholars believe that Paul used this letter as his model for his letter to the Ephesians.

Key Themes

Several key themes are prominent in Paul's letter to the Colossians. The first is that *believers must recognize the preeminence of Christ*. The false teachers were proclaiming that Jesus was *a* god but not *the* highest deity—and certainly not God alone. To counter these claims, Paul reminded the believers of Christ's preeminence in their lives, His preeminence in His nature and work, His preeminence over false religions, and His preeminence in Christian living. He also reminded them that Jesus is head over the church (see Colossians 1:9–18).

A second theme is that *believers in Christ must hold fast to the truth of the gospel.* Paul was concerned the Colossians would be persuaded by the wisdom of the false teachings and their arguments grounded in human wisdom. For this reason, he urged the believers to remember that Christ was the only source of true wisdom—as the one in which "are hidden all the treasures of wisdom and knowledge" (see 2:1–9). The believers needed to remember who they were in Christ and not be taken in by teachings that demanded they needed to follow certain rites and rituals in order to be saved (see 2:10–23).

A third theme is that *believers in Christ must put aside the "old man" and embrace the "new man."* Paul used this language to demonstrate the difference between the believers' former lives and the transformation that had now taken place with them. He calls out the characteristics of the "old man," which include anger, blasphemy, filthy language, and lying. He contrasts those traits with the characteristics of the "new man"—the people they now are in Christ—which include kindness, humility, long-suffering, and forgiveness (see 3:1–17). Based on these traits, Paul then sketched the roles family members played in creating a God-honoring dynamic of love, obedience, submission, and accountability in the home (see 3:18–25).

PHILEMON

Author and Date

The author of this letter also identifies himself as Paul, and his opening words indicate that he was again collaborating with his associate Timothy (see 1:1). The lists of companions cited in both letters are nearly identical, and it is clear that both were delivered together by the same individuals.

Early church leaders such Tertullian (c. AD 210) and Origen (c. AD 240) recognized the apostle Paul as its author, and there is no compelling evidence that anyone else penned its content. Most scholars today see Philemon and Colossians as "companion" letters, written at approximately the same time, while Paul was imprisoned in Rome (c. AD 60).

Background and Setting

It is believed that the apostle Paul was in prison when he came into contact with a slave named Onesimus. He learned that this man had wronged his master, a leader in the church in Colossae named Philemon, and then fled to escape the consequences. Paul took an interest in Onesimus and likely was responsible for leading him to Christ. He then instructed Onesimus to return to his master and carry this letter back with him. Interestingly, Paul addressed this letter not only to Philemon but also to "Apphia, Archippus . . . and to the church" (1:2), which indicates that he viewed the matter not merely as personal but as one that involved the entire congregation. Paul's appeal in the letter is for both Philemon and the church to accept Onesimus—whom he now views as his "son" (see 1:10)—back into their fellowship as a "beloved brother" (1:16).

Key Themes

Several key themes are prominent in Paul's letter to Philemon. The first is that *believers in Christ are called to intercede for one another.* Paul not only interceded for the believers in Colossae in his prayers (see 1:4) but also personally took up the cause of Onesimus (see 1:10). This leads to a second main theme—*believers in Christ are to forgive one another.* Paul urged Philemon and the entire congregation in Colossae to forgive and accept Onesimus back into their fellowship—not as a runaway *slave* but as a Christian *brother.* He even encouraged Philemon to bill *him* for the expenses that Onesimus had incurred when he fled, adding a subtle reminder of the debt that Philemon owed him for leading him to Christ (see 1:18–19).

KEY APPLICATIONS

The letter of Colossians reveals that *we need to fill up our vision with Christ*. We must take the time—and *make* the time—to consider who Christ is in our lives and what He has done for us. When life gets confusing, we need to push aside our nagging worries and lock our gaze on God's Son. This is more than just an intellectual exercise, for the more we *focus* on Jesus, the more we *become* like Him. The letter of Philemon reveals that *we need to forgive others as God has forgiven u*s. We are all, in one way or another, running from God. We all have a debt we cannot repay—a debt caused by our sin that leads to death. But through Christ, we have been set free. Now, just as we have received that gift of forgiveness, we must extend it to others. Christian forgiveness must know no boundaries! It should be made available to all who seek it.

SINGING THE PRAISES OF THE UNSUNG

Colossians 1:1–8

GETTING STARTED

Who is someone you admire for the work he or she is doing in the body of Christ? What do you admire most about that person?

_____

_____

_____

_____

_____

_____

_____

_____

_____

_____

_____

_____

_____

_____

_____

_____

_____

_____

SETTING THE STAGE

The city of Colossae was located in the Roman province of Asia (modern-day Turkey) near the Lycus River. It had once been a populous and wealthy city, famous for its wool trade, but by the time of the apostle Paul it had diminished in both size and significance. Furthermore, unlike most of the other cities we read about in the New Testament, it appears that Paul had never set foot within its limits. Rather, he had only "heard of" the Colossian believers' faith (1:4).

The person who had actually been responsible for bringing the gospel to Colossae and planting a church there appears to have been a man named Epaphras. The apostle Paul uses two phrases in the New Testament to describe this individual, each of which helps us to understand why God chose to use him for His plans. First, Paul calls Epaphras his "dear fellow servant" (Colossians 1:7). The word *dear* tells us that Epaphras was beloved. The word *fellow* reveals that he was not isolated or a loner. The word *servant* tells us about his attitude. There was nothing that Epaphras would not do to serve the cause of Christ.

Later, Paul adds that Epaphras was "a bondservant" (Colossians 4:12). In his writings, the apostle uses this phrase to describe only one other person besides himself: his co-worker Timothy (see Philippians 1:1). A *bondservant* was attached to his master. Paul thought of himself as a bondservant—a slave—of Jesus Christ. There was nothing he would not do for Christ because he was *bound* to Christ. Thus, in calling Epaphras a "servant" and "bondservant," Paul is saying that Epaphras cared for the things of Christ far more than for his own position or possessions. He ministered in humility, not seeking praise or recognition.

We can learn much from this man . . . even though all we know about him is found in just these few verses! We can say, "If God, by His grace and mercy, could use Epaphras in such a powerful way, perhaps He can use me." This is the joy found in studying the Word of God! It helps us to enter into the joy of the Lord, because we realize that we are all equally loved and called by God to join Him in reconciling the world to Himself.

EXPLORING THE TEXT

Paul's Greeting (Colossians 1:1–4)

> ¹ Paul, an apostle of Jesus Christ by the will of God, and Timothy our brother,
>
> ² To the saints and faithful brethren in Christ who are in Colossae:
>
> Grace to you and peace from God our Father and the Lord Jesus Christ.
>
> ³ We give thanks to the God and Father of our Lord Jesus Christ, praying always for you, ⁴ since we heard of your faith in Christ Jesus and of your love for all the saints . . .

1. The word *apostle* has multiple uses in Scripture. It refers not only to one of the twelve disciples (see Acts 1:26) but also to a messenger of the gospel (see Philippians 2:25). Paul's use of it in this passage refers to his specific calling. What did he want the believers in Colossae to understand about that calling (see Colossians 1:1)?

_____

_____

_____

_____

_____

_____

_____

_____

_____

_____

_____

_____

2. Paul had heard reports of the Colossian church from Epaphras. What did he hear about the Colossian believers that made him so thankful (see verses 3–4)?

_____

_____

_____

_____

_____

_____

Their Faith in Christ (Colossians 1:5–8)

> [5] . . . because of the hope which is laid up for you in heaven, of which you heard before in the word of the truth of the gospel, [6] which has come to you, as it has also in all the world, and is bringing forth fruit, as it is also among you since the day you heard and knew the grace of God in truth; [7] as you also learned from Epaphras, our dear fellow servant, who is a faithful minister of Christ on your behalf, [8] who also declared to us your love in the Spirit.

3. How does the apostle Paul describe the gospel that the believers in Colossae received? What impact was the message of that gospel having on their lives (see verses 5–6)?

_____

_____

_____

_____

_____

_____

_____

4. How does Paul describe the work that Epaphras has done in their community? What had this "dear fellow servant" and "faithful minister" declared about them to Paul (see verse 7)?

_____

_____

_____

_____

_____

_____

_____

_____

_____

GOING DEEPER

Paul understood how important it was to have trustworthy individuals like Epaphras in positions of church leadership. The apostle's constant concern was that new believers would be persuaded to turn away from the "truth of the gospel" (Colossians 1:5) and follow a "different gospel" (Galatians 1:6). For this reason, he saw the bar high for those who desired to be leaders in the church. We find some of these qualifications listed in his first letter to Timothy.

Qualifications of Overseers (1 Timothy 3:2–7)

² A bishop then must be blameless, the husband of one wife, temperate, sober-minded, of good behavior, hospitable, able to teach; ³ not given to wine, not violent, not greedy for money, but gentle, not quarrelsome, not covetous; ⁴ one who rules his own house well, having his children in submission with all reverence. ⁵ (For if a man does not know how to rule his own house, how will he take care of the church of God?); ⁶ not a novice, lest being puffed up with pride

he fall into the same condemnation as the devil. [7] Moreover he must have a good testimony among those who are outside, lest he fall into reproach and the snare of the devil.

---

5. What are some of the positive qualities that Paul says a bishop (or "overseer") in the church must possess? What are some of the negative traits that he must avoid (see verses 2–5)?

_____

_____

_____

_____

_____

_____

_____

6. What was the danger in allowing a person who was a novice (literally "newly planted") to have a position of church leadership? Why was it important for leaders to have a good reputation in the local community (see verses 6–7)?

_____

_____

_____

_____

_____

_____

_____

_____

Qualifications of Deacons (1 Timothy 3:8–12)

> [8] Likewise deacons must be reverent, not double-tongued, not given to much wine, not greedy for money, [9] holding the mystery of the faith with a pure conscience. [10] But let these also first be tested; then let them serve as deacons, being found blameless. [11] Likewise, their wives must be reverent, not slanderers, temperate, faithful in all things. [12] Let deacons be the husbands of one wife, ruling their children and their own houses well.

7. Deacons were servants or ministers who worked directly under the bishops in the church. What specific qualities did these individuals need to possess (see verses 8–9)?

_____

_____

_____

_____

_____

_____

_____

8. What does Paul say about the deacons' home life (see verse 12)? Why do you think he was so particular about stressing these points?

_____

_____

_____

_____

_____

_____

_____

REVIEWING THE STORY

Paul identifies himself as an apostle *chosen* by God. He establishes his credentials upfront so there will be no questioning of the teachings that follow. He is saying, in essence, "This is not me talking—this is God." Paul refers to Timothy and Epaphras in a show of appreciation for their friendship and support for their ministry. In a culture rife with false teachers, Paul wants the Colossians to know whom they can trust. He assures them that he is continuously praying for them and giving thanks to God for the fruits of ministry he sees in them.

9. What two blessings does Paul offer the Colossian believers (see Colossians 1:2)?

_____

_____

_____

_____

_____

_____

10. For what two things do Paul and his fellow ministers give thanks to God regarding the Colossian Christians (see Colossians 1:2)?

_____

_____

_____

_____

_____

_____

_____

_____

11. How does Paul describe the hope of the Colossian believers (see Colossians 1:5)?

_____

_____

_____

_____

_____

_____

_____

_____

_____

_____

_____

_____

12. When did the gospel begin to make a difference in the believers' lives (see Colossians 1:6)?

_____

_____

_____

_____

_____

_____

_____

_____

_____

_____

_____

_____

APPLYING THE MESSAGE

13. What comes to mind when you consider "the hope which is laid up for you in heaven" (Colossians 1:5)? How would you describe the impact of that hope in your life?

_____

_____

_____

_____

_____

_____

_____

_____

_____

_____

_____

14. What type of "fruit" are you producing for God's kingdom? What would people say about your work in the body of Christ if they were mentioning you in a letter?

_____

_____

_____

_____

_____

_____

_____

_____

_____

REFLECTING ON THE MEANING

In the opening verses of Colossians, Paul mentions Epaphras, "a faithful minister of Christ" (1:7). In the body of Christ, many of us are like Epaphras. We work behind the scenes, doing the necessary things that make ministry work. Because our work is unglamorous, it can be taken for granted—and frequently is. If we are not careful, the enemy can use that to discourage us and lessen our ministry impact. So how do we survive and thrive out of the ministry spotlight?

First, we remind ourselves about who is the focus of our ministry. In 2 Corinthians 4:5, the apostle Paul writes, "For we do not preach ourselves, but Christ Jesus the Lord, and ourselves your bondservants for Jesus' sake." We don't need to be recognized in order for our ministry to be important. It is already important by virtue of the fact that it is the Lord's work.

Second, we think in terms of the body of Christ. No part of the body is more important than another. Paul makes this clear in 1 Corinthians 12:20–22 when he writes, "There are many members, yet one body. And the eye cannot say to the hand, 'I have no need of you'; nor again the head to the feet, 'I have no need of you.' No, much rather, those members of the body which seem to be weaker are necessary." Our goal is not to promote our status as a hand or foot but rather to do everything in our power to help the entire body function properly.

Third, we encourage others whose ministry in the church might otherwise go overlooked. As Paul wrote in 1 Thessalonians 5:12–13, "We urge you, brethren, to recognize those who labor among you . . . and to esteem them very highly in love for their work's sake." Through a card or a conversation, we can express our heartfelt gratitude for their work. We can remember those people in our prayers and ask God to bless their work.

As we do these things, we will show that we are "faithful ministers" of Christ to our local fellowship, just as Epaphras was a faithful minister to his church community in Colossae.

JOURNALING YOUR RESPONSE

What is the most encouraging thing someone could say to you about your Christian ministry?

WISDOM AND UNDERSTANDING

Colossians 1:9–18

GETTING STARTED

When was the last time you asked the Lord for wisdom? What was the outcome of that prayer?

_____

_____

_____

_____

_____

_____

_____

_____

_____

_____

_____

_____

_____

_____

_____

_____

_____

_____

SETTING THE STAGE

In this section of Paul's letter, we find his personal prayer for the Colossian believers. The apostle begins the prayer with these words: "For this reason we also, since the day we heard it, do not cease to pray for you, and to ask that you may be filled with the knowledge of His will in all wisdom and spiritual understanding" (Colossians 1:9). God's desire is for His followers to be filled with His wisdom and gain greater spiritual understanding.

This is His desire for us today as well—and we gain this wisdom and understanding through the pages of God's Word. Sadly, the reality is that too few of God's people today take this book seriously and allow its teaching to shape their spiritual understanding. In the United States, surveys have shown that a majority of people believe the Bible to be the inspired Word of God. Many claim that they read the Bible at least monthly. But very few could even name one of the four Gospels! And even fewer could say who delivered the Sermon on the Mount.

Today, the Bible is available in more than 1,800 languages, and most of us have more than one translation in our homes. But none of this mere access to God's wisdom will lead us to greater spiritual maturity in Christ unless we choose to *actually* access that content! For it is only when we open the pages of our Bible and seek to understand God's truth that we discover how to "walk worthy of the Lord, fully pleasing Him, being fruitful in every good work and increasing in the knowledge of God; strengthened with all might" (Colossians 1:10–11).

EXPLORING THE TEXT

Paul's Thanksgiving and Prayer (Colossians 1:9–14)

⁹ For this reason we also, since the day we heard it, do not cease to pray for you, and to ask that you may be filled with the knowledge of His will in all wisdom and spiritual understanding; ¹⁰ that you may walk worthy of the Lord, fully pleasing Him, being fruitful in every

good work and increasing in the knowledge of God; [11] strengthened with all might, according to His glorious power, for all patience and longsuffering with joy; [12] giving thanks to the Father who has qualified us to be partakers of the inheritance of the saints in the light. [13] He has delivered us from the power of darkness and conveyed us into the kingdom of the Son of His love, [14] in whom we have redemption through His blood, the forgiveness of sin.

---

1. Paul wholeheartedly sought to please the Lord (see 2 Corinthians 5:9), and he desired that the Colossian believers would do the same. For this reason, Paul prays that they would "be filled with the knowledge" of God's will (Colossians 1:9). What does he state will be the results when believers are filled with this knowledge of God's will (see verses 9–12)?

2. Paul had opened his letter with an explanation of why he was thankful for the Colossian believers (see verses 4–5). In this section, he now urges the Colossians to be thankful as well. For what reason does Paul say the believers can be thankful (see verses 12–14)?

_____

_____

_____

_____

_____

_____

_____

_____

_____

_____

_____

_____

_____

_____

_____

_____

The Firstborn Over All Creation (Colossians 1:15–18)

[15] He is the image of the invisible God, the firstborn over all creation. [16] For by Him all things were created that are in heaven and that are on earth, visible and invisible, whether thrones or dominions or principalities or powers. All things were created through Him and for Him. [17] And He is before all things, and in Him all things consist. [18] And He is the head of the body, the church, who is the beginning, the firstborn from the dead, that in all things He may have the preeminence.

3. Paul, like the other Jews of his day, believed that God was invisible. He also believed that it was idolatrous to try to portray God with a statue or image (see Romans 1:22–23). Rather, how does Paul say, in this passage regarding the pre-eminence of Christ, that believers are able to see the "image" of God (see verses 15–16)?

_____

_____

_____

_____

_____

_____

_____

_____

_____

4. The disciple John wrote, "All things were made through [Christ], and without Him nothing was made that was made" (John 1:3). What does Paul say about God's creative work through Christ? Over what has Jesus been given authority (see Colossians 1:16–18)?

_____

_____

_____

_____

_____

_____

_____

_____

_____

GOING DEEPER

Paul was not the only New Testament writer to emphasize the importance of *living* the principles found in God's Word. In the epistle of James, we find the author likewise urging his readers to not simply *hear* the word of God but to actually put what they hear into *practice*. James is clear that those who fail to act on what they receive are merely deceiving themselves.

Listening and Doing (James 1:21–24)

[21] Therefore lay aside all filthiness and overflow of wickedness, and receive with meekness the implanted word, which is able to save your souls.

[22] But be doers of the word, and not hearers only, deceiving yourselves. [23] For if anyone is a hearer of the word and not a doer, he is like a man observing his natural face in a mirror; [24] for he observes himself, goes away, and immediately forgets what kind of man he was.

5. How does James say that believers in Christ are to receive God's Word? What power does the truth of God contain as it relates to our lives (see verse 21)?

6. What important next step must we take after receiving God's Word? What is the difference between being a *hearer* of the Word and a *doer* of the Word (see verses 22–24)?

_____

_____

_____

_____

_____

_____

_____

_____

_____

_____

_____

_____

_____

_____

_____

_____

_____

Pure and Undefiled Religion (James 1:25–27)

25 But he who looks into the perfect law of liberty and continues in it, and is not a forgetful hearer but a doer of the work, this one will be blessed in what he does.

26 If anyone among you thinks he is religious, and does not bridle his tongue but deceives his own heart, this one's religion is useless.

27 Pure and undefiled religion before God and the Father is this: to visit orphans and widows in their trouble, and to keep oneself unspotted from the world.

7. James says that those who hear the Word of God but do not allow it to transform their lives only deceive themselves, because the truth of God's Word does not reside within them. But what happens when we are faithful "doers" of the Word (see verse 25)?

8. What does being a true doer of the Word look like in action? How do you think this constitutes "pure and undefiled religion" before God (see verses 26–27)?

REVIEWING THE STORY

Paul prays for the Colossians to have more than an intellectual understanding of God and His Word. He asks that they have a true knowledge of God that produces spiritual wisdom in their lives. He prays the Colossians will be filled with the fullness of God in Christ and that they will conduct their lives in a way worthy of the Lord. He urges them to embrace a spirit of joy and gratitude because God has qualified them to share in the inheritance of the saints, rescued them from darkness, and transferred them into the kingdom of Christ.

9. What does the knowledge of God and His Word strengthen us for (see Colossians 1:11)?

_____

_____

_____

_____

_____

_____

_____

10. What do we have in Christ (see Colossians 1:14)?

_____

_____

_____

_____

_____

_____

_____

11. In Jewish culture, the firstborn son received a double portion of the inheritance and was given authority in the family. How does this apply to Christ (see Colossians 1:15)?

_____

_____

_____

_____

_____

12. How does the apostle Paul describe Jesus' role in the church (see Colossians 1:18)?

_____

_____

_____

_____

_____

APPLYING THE MESSAGE

13. What are some practices you have employed to increase your _knowledge_ of God's Word?

_____

_____

_____

_____

_____

_____

14. What are some strategies you have employed to ensure that you are actually putting that knowledge of God's Word into *practice*?

_____

_____

_____

_____

REFLECTING ON THE MEANING

Paul prayed the Colossians would "be filled with the knowledge of [God's] will in all wisdom and spiritual understanding" (Colossians 1:9). Often we fill our minds with the truth of the Word of God, but the spiritual understanding part escapes us. We acquire the information, but we fail to gain spiritual understanding because we fail to apply that knowledge to our lives.

However, in verse 10, Paul outlines three benefits that we receive when we choose to put God's Word into practice. First, *we please God continuously*. When we study the Word of God, we develop an understanding of what truly pleases Him. This knowledge enables us to then "work worthy of the Lord" by putting it into practice. The better we know the Lord, the better we know what pleases Him. Our goal, according to Paul's prayer, is to know Jesus so well that we can walk according to His will.

Second, *we produce fruit constantly*. Fruit, in this respect, represents our character (what we are), our conduct (what we do), our conversation (what we say), our contributions (what we give), and our converts (who we win for Christ). When the Word of God is dwelling in our hearts, we are not just reading it to see what it says but to determine what we should do. When we start living in this manner, we become productive in every area of our lives.

Third, *we progress in knowledge continuously*. When we put the Word of God into practice, we grow in spiritual maturity. When we come to a crisis that forces us to choose between what somebody else wants and what God wants, we choose God's will—knowing we can trust in Him. In doing so, our decision becomes a part of our spiritual being.

We receive all of these benefits—*pleasing God, producing fruit,* and *progressing in knowledge*—when we continually choose to put God's Word into practice. Furthermore, we discover that as we do, we are "strengthened with all [of God's] might" (verse 11).

JOURNALING YOUR RESPONSE

In what area of life right now do you need greater wisdom and understanding from God?

_____

_____

_____

_____

_____

_____

_____

_____

_____

_____

_____

_____

_____

_____

_____

_____

_____

_____

_____

_____

LESSON *three*

THE FULLNESS OF CHRIST

Colossians 1:19–29

GETTING STARTED

Why is it important that Jesus was both fully human and fully divine?

_____

_____

_____

_____

_____

_____

_____

_____

_____

_____

_____

_____

_____

_____

_____

_____

_____

_____

_____

_____

_____

_____

SETTING THE STAGE

The idea of God's dwelling with His people was nothing new to Jewish believers. It was an integral part of their history and national identity. God had led their ancestors across the wilderness, from Egypt to Canaan, in the form of a cloud by day and a pillar of fire by night. His presence had dwelled in the Most Holy Place—the most sacred part of the Jewish tabernacle.

The Jewish people were thus accustomed to the idea of God's spiritual presence dwelling in their midst. While they could not see Him, touch Him, or (aside from a few occasions) hear Him, they knew He was there. So they were careful to observe the rules and restrictions that His presence demanded.

However, as Paul notes in this next section of Colossians, God took the concept of dwelling with His people one step further when He sent His Son into the world. Jesus took on human form and *became* one of us. The Creator lived among His creation, in a physical body, for thirty-three years. He laid aside His divine attributes of omnipresence and squeezed Himself into a container of flesh. He allowed people to see, hear, smell, and touch Him. He made Himself vulnerable to pain, suffering, and death. He took on human frailty in order to save us.

The apostle Paul recognized this was a difficult concept for people to grasp. It was also a source of ammunition for his opponents. The false teachers in the Colossian church had certainly seized on the concept of the incarnation to plant seeds of doubt in the minds of the believers. They had tried to convince the Colossians that only a *spiritual* being could offer salvation. Jesus was only *human*, they claimed, so He could not be their Savior.

Paul sets out to refute this argument by showing how both Jesus' divinity *and* humanity were necessary for God's plan of salvation. Jesus had to be fully divine: "It pleased the Father that in Him all the fullness should dwell" (Colossians 1:19). But He also had to be fully human: "[God] has reconciled in the body of [Jesus'] flesh through death, to present you holy, and blameless, and above reproach in His sight" (verses 21–22). Divinity *and* humanity. Both were necessary for Christ to be able to offer the supreme sacrifice for our sins.

EXPLORING THE TEXT

Reconciled in Christ (Colossians 1:19–23)

¹⁹ For it pleased the Father that in Him all the fullness should dwell, ²⁰ and by Him to reconcile all things to Himself, by Him, whether things on earth or things in heaven, having made peace through the blood of His cross.

²¹ And you, who once were alienated and enemies in your mind by wicked works, yet now He has reconciled ²² in the body of His flesh through death, to present you holy, and blameless, and above reproach in His sight—²³ if indeed you continue in the faith, grounded and steadfast, and are not moved away from the hope of the gospel which you heard, which was preached to every creature under heaven, of which I, Paul, became a minister.

1. Paul has just stated that Jesus "is the head of the body, the church, who is the beginning, the firstborn from the dead, that in all things He may have the preeminence" (verse 18). He now continues this line of reasoning to show why the resurrected Christ reigns supreme. What does Paul say it "pleased the Father" to do through the person of Christ? What did Jesus accomplish through His death on the cross and His resurrection (see verses 19–20)?

2. How do believers remain "grounded and steadfast" in their faith (see Colossians 1:21–23)?

_____

_____

_____

_____

_____

_____

_____

_____

_____

_____

Sacrificial Service for Christ (Colossians 1:24–29)

24 I now rejoice in my sufferings for you, and fill up in my flesh what is lacking in the afflictions of Christ, for the sake of His body, which is the church, 25 of which I became a minister according to the stewardship from God which was given to me for you, to fulfill the word of God, 26 the mystery which has been hidden from ages and from generations, but now has been revealed to His saints. 27 To them God willed to make known what are the riches of the glory of this mystery among the Gentiles: which is Christ in you, the hope of glory. 28 Him we preach, warning every man and teaching every man in all wisdom, that we may present every man perfect in Christ Jesus. 29 To this end I also labor, striving according to His working which works in me mightily.

3. Although Paul does not describe his specific sufferings in these verses, we know from other passages in Scripture that he suffered much affliction for the sake of the gospel (see, for example, 2 Corinthians

11:23–27). What is Paul's attitude toward the trials and tribulations that he endured as a follower of Christ (see Colossians 1:24–25)?

_____

_____

_____

_____

_____

_____

4. The "mystery" to which Paul refers in this passage pertains to Jesus. God's plan to send His Son into the world as the Messiah had been "hidden from ages and from generations" (verse 26). What does Paul now say had been revealed to the saints of God—which included the Gentile believers like those in Colossae (see verses 27–28)?

_____

_____

_____

_____

_____

GOING DEEPER

Paul closes this section of Colossians by noting the purpose of his mission: "[Christ] we preach, warning every man and teaching every man in all wisdom, that we may present every man perfect in Christ Jesus" (Colossians 1:28). The apostle well understood that this process of perfection did not occur instantaneously or automatically in people. In fact, in his letter to the Philippians, he confirmed that he also faced this continuous process of growing in his faith. Although he had accomplished much, he knew there was still much work to be done.

Pressing Toward the Goal (Philippians 3:12–16)

¹² Not that I have already attained, or am already perfected; but I press on, that I may lay hold of that for which Christ Jesus has also laid hold of me. ¹³ Brethren, I do not count myself to have apprehended; but one thing I do, forgetting those things which are behind and reaching forward to those things which are ahead, ¹⁴ I press toward the goal for the prize of the upward call of God in Christ Jesus.

¹⁵ Therefore let us, as many as are mature, have this mind; and if in anything you think otherwise, God will reveal even this to you. ¹⁶ Nevertheless, to the degree that we have already attained, let us walk by the same rule, let us be of the same mind.

5. Paul's use of the word "call" in verse 14 suggests a ceremony at the end of a race, in which the winner was summoned to an elevated judge's stand to receive a prize. What was Paul's strategy for receiving such a call (see verses 12–14)?

_____

_____

_____

_____

_____

6. Paul adds a cautionary note about any believer who might think that he or she has already "arrived" at the goal. What advice does he give to such individuals (see verses 15–16)?

_____

_____

_____

_____

The author of the book of Hebrews also begins his letter by glorifying Christ as the supreme revelation of God. The author is also careful to point out that Jesus, being God in the flesh, is exalted above even the angels. Like Paul, he sees Jesus as a member of the Godhead.

God's Supreme Revelation (Hebrews 1:1–9)

[1] God, who at various times and in various ways spoke in time past to the fathers by the prophets, [2] has in these last days spoken to us by His Son, whom He has appointed heir of all things, through whom also He made the worlds; [3] who being the brightness of His glory and the express image of His person, and upholding all things by the word of His power, when He had by Himself purged our sins, sat down at the right hand of the Majesty on high, [4] having become so much better than the angels, as He has by inheritance obtained a more excellent name than they.

[5] For to which of the angels did He ever say:

"You are My Son,
Today I have begotten You"?

And again:

"I will be to Him a Father,
And He shall be to Me a Son"?

[6] But when He again brings the firstborn into the world, He says:

"Let all the angels of God worship Him."

[7] And of the angels He says:

"Who makes His angels spirits
And His ministers a flame of fire." . . .

[8] But to the Son He says:

"Your throne, O God, is forever and ever;
A scepter of righteousness is the scepter of Your kingdom.
[9] You have loved righteousness and hated lawlessness;
Therefore God, Your God, has anointed You
With the oil of gladness more than Your companions."

---

7. During Old Testament times, God communicated His laws, instructions, warnings, and blessings to His people through His prophets. In what way has Jesus replaced the Old Testament prophets? How is Jesus superior to the prophets (see verses 1–3)?

_____

_____

_____

_____

_____

8. Much of the book of Hebrews focuses on Jesus' superiority to all created beings and human institutions. The author wants his readers to understand Jesus' position of authority as the Son of God. In what ways is Jesus superior to the angels? What does the author of Hebrews say about the throne that Jesus inhabits (see verses 4–9)?

_____

_____

_____

_____

_____

REVIEWING THE STORY

Paul helps the Colossian believers understand that Jesus was fully divine but also fully human. Jesus was fully God, and all "the fullness" of God dwelt in Him. Yet Jesus was also fully human, and it is because of His physical death on the cross that reconciliation with God is possible. Paul goes on to note this is the gospel he proclaims—and that he can even rejoice in his sufferings to proclaim it. Paul closes by making it clear to the Colossian believers that the work he does on the Lord's behalf is only made possible by the Lord's work in his own life.

9. What was necessary in order for us to have peace with God (see Colossians 1:19–20)?

_____

_____

_____

10. What was our status with God before Jesus reconciled us (see Colossians 1:21)?

_____

_____

_____

_____

11. What was Paul's reaction to the suffering he experienced while doing the work and will of the Lord (see Colossians 1:24)?

_____

_____

_____

_____

12. Where did Paul find the strength and endurance to labor for the Lord (see Colossians 1:29)?

APPLYING THE MESSAGE

13. What are some of the sacrifices that you have made in your service to Christ?

14. What results have you seen in other people's lives because of the sacrifices you made?

REFLECTING ON THE MEANING

The apostle Paul concludes this section of Colossians with what could be considered his mission statement: "[Christ] we preach, warning every man and teaching every man in all wisdom, that we may present every man perfect in Christ Jesus" (1:28). At first glance, Paul's use of the word *perfect* can feel intimidating. After all, we cannot set the bar any higher than at perfection! Furthermore, we all are only too aware of our *imperfection*. We know we can't be perfect—that it is simply an impossible goal to attain. So why bother even trying?

The good news is that the word translated as *perfect* in this verse means "mature" or "complete." The goal is *not* for us to try and lead mistake-free existences but to continually deepen our relationship with Christ and make a difference for His kingdom. It is to agree to embark on the lifelong process of seeking to continually mature in our faith.

It is herein that lies both the challenge and the opportunity. There will be no moment in life when we will reach complete spiritual maturity. No matter how close to "completion" our faith may seem, there will always be more growing to do and more opportunities available to us to become closer to God and more Christlike in behavior. There is no resting on our laurels.

By the same token, there is also nothing that can disqualify us from our pursuit of perfection. All spiritual journeys include lulls, setbacks, and valleys along the way. But we need not be discouraged by our less-than-mature spiritual moments. We need only to confess our failures, learn from our mistakes, and continue our journey, a little wiser from the experience.

Our goal is to become mature and complete followers of Christ. We do this by reading God's Word and applying it to our lives, making prayer and quiet time a daily priority, and looking for ways to bring glory to God in our daily interactions. We do this by sacrificing our comfort for the sake of others, having a heart for the lost and the needy, and maintaining an ever-growing circle of friends for support in the body of Christ. As we seek to do each of these things, we move once step closer toward the end goal of being "perfect" in our faith.

JOURNALING YOUR RESPONSE

What do you need to do *today* to move one step closer in becoming "perfect" in your faith?

TRUE OR FALSE?

Colossians 2:1–10

GETTING STARTED

What false teaching has proved to be a stumbling block for you or someone you love?

_____

_____

_____

_____

_____

_____

_____

_____

_____

_____

_____

_____

_____

_____

_____

_____

_____

_____

_____

_____

SETTING THE STAGE

The false teachers who had infiltrated the church in Colossae had one undeniable advantage over the apostle Paul: they were in Colossae. They could command the Colossian believers' attention. They could persuade them with their polished speeches and their promises of giving the Colossians a higher level of spiritual knowledge. They could sow seeds of doubt and confusion without being challenged by a formidable opponent.

Travel to Colossae—or anywhere else, for that matter—was not a luxury that Paul enjoyed when he wrote his letter to the Colossians. As we have discussed, the apostle was under house arrest in Rome at the time, and his movements were extremely limited. When he later asks the Colossians to "remember my chains" (4:18), he is not asking for their sympathy or their pity. Rather, he is simply reminding them why he cannot visit them.

Another disadvantage was that Paul had never visited the Colossian church. He had a personal history with only a few of its members. So he couldn't appeal to their shared ministry experiences. He couldn't draw on what he knew about them personally to make his case. Still, he was concerned about the wellbeing of this community—and also its sister congregation in nearby Laodicea. In fact, Paul makes it clear his letter is intended to be shared with the Laodicean believers, who, in turn, would share their own letter with the Colossian Christians.

Paul wants to do for both congregations with his letter what he could not do in person: equip them to recognize and reject the false teaching that was in their midst.

EXPLORING THE TEXT

Not Philosophy but Christ (Colossians 2:1–5)

> [1] For I want you to know what a great conflict I have for you and those in Laodicea, and for as many as have not seen my face in the flesh,
> [2] that their hearts may be encouraged, being knit together in love, and

attaining to all riches of the full assurance of understanding, to the knowledge of the mystery of God, both of the Father and of Christ, ³ in whom are hidden all the treasures of wisdom and knowledge.

⁴ Now this I say lest anyone should deceive you with persuasive words. ⁵ For though I am absent in the flesh, yet I am with you in spirit, rejoicing to see your good order and the steadfastness of your faith in Christ.

---

1. As previously noted, Paul did not start the church in Colossae or the church in Laodicea, and he had never met most of the people in those churches. Given this fact, what did he want them to understand about him and his ministry (see verses 1–3)?

_____

_____

_____

_____

_____

2. It appears that some of the believers in the Colossian church had been persuaded by the false teachers' eloquent speech and arguments. Where does Paul say the true source of wisdom and knowledge lies? What does he encourage them to do (see verses 3–5)?

_____

_____

_____

_____

_____

_____

Walk in Him (Colossians 2:6–10)

⁶ As you therefore have received Christ Jesus the Lord, so walk in Him, ⁷ rooted and built up in Him and established in the faith, as you have been taught, abounding in it with thanksgiving.

⁸ Beware lest anyone cheat you through philosophy and empty deceit, according to the tradition of men, according to the basic principles of the world, and not according to Christ. ⁹ For in Him dwells all the fullness of the Godhead bodily; ¹⁰ and you are complete in Him, who is the head of all principality and power.

3. The Colossian believers had taken the first steps by receiving Christ, confessing Him, and being baptized. But Paul wanted them to continue making strides in their spiritual maturity. What does he instruct them to do next in this regard (see verses 6–7)?

_____

_____

_____

_____

_____

_____

_____

_____

_____

_____

_____

_____

_____

_____

4. Paul warns the Colossians believers to exercise caution in their walk with Christ, especially as they faced worldly philosophies with their empty deceit. What clues does he offer for recognizing those teachings that are built on empty deceit (see verses 8–10)?

_____

_____

_____

_____

_____

_____

_____

_____

_____

_____

GOING DEEPER

The city of Colossae was located 120 miles east of Ephesus and lay in close proximity to two other major cities: Laodicea and Hierapolis. The city of Hierapolis is only mentioned once in the New Testament (see Colossians 4:13), and nothing is known about the church there. However, the apostle John lists Laodicea as one of the "seven churches" to whom he was instructed to write a letter in the book of Revelation. John's message reveals a lot about that congregation and the issues that they—like the Colossians—were facing in their journey with Christ.

The Lukewarm Church (Revelation 3:14–22)

[14] "And to the angel of the church of the Laodiceans write,

'These things says the Amen, the Faithful and True Witness, the Beginning of the creation of God: [15] "I know your works, that you are neither cold nor hot. I could wish you were cold or hot. [16] So then, because you are lukewarm, and neither cold nor hot, I will vomit

41

you out of My mouth. [17] Because you say, 'I am rich, have become wealthy, and have need of nothing'—and do not know that you are wretched, miserable, poor, blind, and naked . . .'"

---

5. The city of Laodicea did not have its own water source, so water from springs south of the city had to travel in from a six-mile-long aqueduct to reach the inhabitants. By the time the water got there, its temperature was lukewarm, rendering it tasteless and unappealing. Why is lukewarm water a fitting description for the church in Laodicea (see verse 14–15)?

_____

_____

_____

_____

_____

_____

_____

_____

6. What did Jesus, the author of this message, say would happen to the Laodiceans because of their "lukewarmness"? What misguided beliefs did they hold (see verses 16–18)?

_____

_____

_____

_____

_____

_____

_____

_____

The Lukewarm Church (Revelation 3:14–22)

[18] "'I counsel you to buy from Me gold refined in the fire, that you may be rich; and white garments, that you may be clothed, that the shame of your nakedness may not be revealed; and anoint your eyes with eye salve, that you may see. [19] As many as I love, I rebuke and chasten. Therefore be zealous and repent. [20] Behold, I stand at the door and knock. If anyone hears My voice and opens the door, I will come in to him and dine with him, and he with Me. [21] To him who overcomes I will grant to sit with Me on My throne, as I also overcame and sat down with My Father on His throne.

[22] "'He who has an ear, let him hear what the Spirit says to the churches.'"

7. What did Jesus counsel the Laodiceans to do? What did He say would happen to the members of the church if they chose to accept His correction (see verses 18–19)?

8. What invitation does Jesus offer to Laodiceans? What promise is contained is the passage for those who choose to respond to His invitation (see verses 20–22)?

_____

_____

_____

_____

_____

_____

_____

REVIEWING THE STORY

Paul had high hopes and expectations for the church in Colossae (and Laodicea). However, in order for them to reach their full potential, the believers had to identify and reject the false teachings that had infiltrated their congregations. So Paul encourages them from a distance. He urges them to examine their beliefs carefully and separate the counterfeit beliefs from the true. He emphasizes they can find completeness only in Christ.

9. What did Paul want for the believers in Colossae, Laodicea, and others whom he not been able to visit in person (see Colossians 2:2)?

_____

_____

_____

_____

_____

_____

_____

10. What qualities in the Colossian believers caused Paul to rejoice (see Colossians 2:5)?

11. What was Paul's warning regarding the philosophies of the world (see Colossians 2:8)?

12. Why do you think Paul emphasizes the authority of Christ (see Colossians 2:10)?

APPLYING THE MESSAGE

13. What steps are you taking in your life right now to be better "rooted and built up in Christ" and "established in the faith" (Colossians 2:7)?

_____

_____

_____

_____

_____

_____

_____

_____

_____

_____

14. How has studying God's Word, spending time in praying, and applying God's wisdom helped you to not be deceived by the "persuasive words" of false teachings?

_____

_____

_____

_____

_____

_____

_____

_____

_____

_____

REFLECTING ON THE MEANING

Paul was concerned that the believers in Colossae were being led astray by human philosophies that sounded true but were false. In this section of Colossians, he seeks to correct this error by reminding the believers of the "treasures of wisdom and knowledge" that they have received in Christ (Colossians 2:3). There are three key principles that surface from his words that you can also apply to your life.

First, remember the gospel that you have received. Paul writes, "As you therefore have received Christ Jesus the Lord, so walk in Him" (verse 6). In your life, you can remember the gospel that you have received by staying diligent in your study of God's Word. You might find it helpful to use a study Bible or commentary, or mark connections between passages, or record what you learn in a journal. The goal is to find out what the text says—and what it *doesn't* say.

Second, remember the community that you have joined. The apostle Paul reminded the Colossian believers that they had been "knit together in love" (verse 2). In the same way, it is important for you to remember that you don't have to "go it alone" in the faith. Seek out trusted believers who can serve as mentors. Join a Bible study group or schedule a monthly meeting with a pastor or church leader—anyone who can answer your questions, guide you, or challenge you to grow. Likewise, you can help to lead others. Don't wait until you "feel ready." Instead, ask God to give you wisdom and courage. Trust the Lord to supply you with all of the resources you need.

Finally, remember the superiority of the God that you serve. The apostle Paul warned the believers in Colossae to avoid "philosophy and empty deceit" and instead heed the One who was "the head of all principality and power" (verses 8, 10). When you recognize the superiority of the gospel, you can challenge any false teaching, while still "speaking the truth in love" (Ephesians 4:15).

Just as Paul did for the Colossians, and for us, you can help others avoid the pitfalls of false teaching.

JOURNALING YOUR RESPONSE

What is one way you can work to increase your familiarity with God's Word this week?

ALIVE IN CHRIST

Colossians 2:11–23

GETTING STARTED

What is your experience with legalism—when people insist that you have to act a certain way in order to be saved?

_____

_____

_____

_____

_____

_____

_____

_____

_____

_____

_____

_____

SETTING THE STAGE

As we noted in the previous lesson, the apostle Paul's primary motive for writing the letter to the Colossians was to combat certain false teachings that had infiltrated the church. Paul has just urged the believers to not trust in eloquent-sounding human philosophies but to look solely to the gospel of Christ for guidance on how to live. In this next section, Paul shifts his focus to another "challenger" that has appeared on the scene. In this case, that challenger is legalism.

Once again, we do not know the specifics related to this false teaching in Colossae. However, from the clues that Paul provides, we can assume the issue at stake was whether Gentile Christians needed to follow the strict observances and dietary restrictions required under Jewish law. This was a common problem in many of Paul's churches. Certain believers from Jewish backgrounds (known as "Judaizers") were known to travel to Gentile churches and proclaim the believers must all follow Jewish practices in order to be considered saved.

Inevitably, the teaching of the Judaizers involved a host of *don'ts*—don't eat that; don't touch that; don't associate with those people. Paul understood the appeal of the message. It offered Gentile believers a measure of control over their spiritual status. It was easier for them to wrap their minds around a system of dos and don'ts that meant they could *earn* their salvation than it was to trust that all they needed to do was put their faith in Christ.

The false teachers were clearly skilled in their presentations. They spoke with intelligence and authority. They knew how to play on the spiritual immaturity of new believers. Paul would have none of it. By employing an equally persuasive set of arguments, he sets out to again affirm that Jesus is superior to all forms of man-made religion. He fortifies the Colossian believers' resolve by assuring them that, in fact, Jesus is everything they need.

EXPLORING THE TEXT

The Circumcision of Christ (Colossians 2:11–17)

---

[11] In Him you were also circumcised with the circumcision made without hands, by putting off the body of the sins of the flesh, by the circumcision of Christ, [12] buried with Him in baptism, in which you

also were raised with Him through faith in the working of God, who raised Him from the dead. ¹³ And you, being dead in your trespasses and the uncircumcision of your flesh, He has made alive together with Him, having forgiven you all trespasses, ¹⁴ having wiped out the handwriting of requirements that was against us, which was contrary to us. And He has taken it out of the way, having nailed it to the cross. ¹⁵ Having disarmed principalities and powers, He made a public spectacle of them, triumphing over them in it.

¹⁶ So let no one judge you in food or in drink, or regarding a festival or a new moon or sabbaths, ¹⁷ which are a shadow of things to come, but the substance is of Christ.

---

1. The Jewish false teachers were evidently making the Gentile believers feel inferior because they had not been circumcised. They prescribed legalistic rules and regulations to prey on the Colossian believers' feelings of inferiority. According to Paul, why did the Colossians have no reason to feel spiritually inferior to anyone (see verses 11–14)?

2. Paul is clear that the rules the Judaizers were imposing were mere shadows of the truth. Christ Himself is the substance. What were Paul's instructions to believers who faced spiritual shaming for not living up to certain expectations (see verses 16–17)?

Not Regulations but Christ (Colossians 2:18–23)

18 Let no one cheat you of your reward, taking delight in false humility and worship of angels, intruding into those things which he has not seen, vainly puffed up by his fleshly mind, 19 and not holding fast to the Head, from whom all the body, nourished and knit together by joints and ligaments, grows with the increase that is from God.

20 Therefore, if you died with Christ from the basic principles of the world, why, as though living in the world, do you subject yourselves to regulations—21 "Do not touch, do not taste, do not handle," 22 which all concern things which perish with the using—according to the commandments and doctrines of men? 23 These things indeed have an appearance of wisdom in self-imposed religion, false humility, and neglect of the body, but are of no value against the indulgence of the flesh.

3. Paul warns the believers to let no one cheat them out of their reward—the gift they have received through their salvation in Christ. What were the false teachers encouraging the believers to take "delight in" instead of Christ? What did Paul encourage them to do so they would not be persuaded by these "vainly puffed up" teachings (see verses 18–19)?

_____

_____

_____

_____

_____

_____

_____

4. Paul urged the Colossians to not abandon Christ by following after legalistic regulations. Elsewhere, the apostle wrote, "For the kingdom of God is not eating and drinking, but righteousness and peace and joy in the Holy Spirit" (Romans 14:17; see also 1 Corinthians 6:13). Why does Paul here say that these false teachings were so harmful to the spiritual health of the Colossian Christians (see Colossians 2:23)?

_____

_____

_____

_____

_____

_____

_____

GOING DEEPER

As we noted, the apostle Paul frequently had to battle against the teachings of the Judaizers, who claimed that Gentile Christians had to follow Jewish practices in order to receive salvation. The believers in the regions of Galatia seem to have especially fallen prey to this form of teaching. In

Paul's letter to these believers, he calls out their foolishness in believing that they can somehow earn their salvation by adhering to the works of the Old Testament law.

Justification by Faith (Galatians 3:1–9)

[1] O foolish Galatians! Who has bewitched you that you should not obey the truth, before whose eyes Jesus Christ was clearly portrayed among you as crucified? [2] This only I want to learn from you: Did you receive the Spirit by the works of the law, or by the hearing of faith? [3] Are you so foolish? Having begun in the Spirit, are you now being made perfect by the flesh? [4] Have you suffered so many things in vain—if indeed it was in vain?

[5] Therefore He who supplies the Spirit to you and works miracles among you, does He do it by the works of the law, or by the hearing of faith?—[6] just as Abraham "believed God, and it was accounted to him for righteousness." [7] Therefore know that only those who are of faith are sons of Abraham. [8] And the Scripture, foreseeing that God would justify the Gentiles by faith, preached the gospel to Abraham beforehand, saying, "In you all the nations shall be blessed." [9] So then those who are of faith are blessed with believing Abraham.

---

5. How does Paul say that the Galatian believers were being "bewitched"? Why does Paul urge them to remember how they came to receive Christ (see verses 1–4)?

_____

_____

_____

_____

_____

_____

6. Paul cites the example of Abraham—a hero of the Jewish faith—to show how he received righteousness not by works but by faith (see verses 6–9). What point was Paul making by citing this example? What is Paul's conclusion about how salvation is obtained?

_____

_____

_____

_____

_____

_____

_____

_____

_____

_____

_____

_____

The Curse Under the Law (Galatians 3:10–14)

¹⁰ For as many as are of the works of the law are under the curse; for it is written, "Cursed is everyone who does not continue in all things which are written in the book of the law, to do them." ¹¹ But that no one is justified by the law in the sight of God is evident, for "the just shall live by faith." ¹² Yet the law is not of faith, but "the man who does them shall live by them."

¹³ Christ has redeemed us from the curse of the law, having become a curse for us (for it is written, "Cursed is everyone who hangs on a tree"), ¹⁴ that the blessing of Abraham might come upon the Gentiles in Christ Jesus, that we might receive the promise of the Spirit through faith.

7. What does Paul say happens to a person who is not able to perfectly live up to the standards of the law? How does this represent a "curse" (see verses 10–12)?

_____

_____

_____

_____

_____

_____

8. How did Jesus resolve the curse of the law? What are we now able to receive (see verses 13–14)?

_____

_____

_____

_____

_____

_____

REVIEWING THE STORY

In embracing Christ, the Colossian believers had broken free from the demands of Judaism. They had experienced the spiritual freedom that Christ's death and resurrection make possible. Why then, Paul asks, were they listening to the false teachers in their midst who were trying to put them under Jewish law? Paul helps the Colossian Christians recognize they were not required to observe Jewish customs such as circumcision and dietary restrictions. He urges them to reject self-imposed religion, false humility, and neglect of their bodies.

9. What is involved in the spiritual circumcision Christ offers that makes it superior to the physical circumcision the false teachers were demanding (see Colossians 2:11–12)?

10. What did Jesus do that the law could not (see Colossians 2:13)?

11. How does Paul describe the way the church should work (see Colossians 2:19)?

12. How did Paul summarize the regulations imposed by the false teachers (see Colossians 2:21)?

_____

_____

_____

_____

APPLYING THE MESSAGE

13. Why might it be tempting to submit to religious rules, regulations, and restrictions?

_____

_____

_____

_____

14. What are some useful techniques you have found in responding to those who promote legalism as a means of "earning" one's salvation?

_____

_____

_____

_____

REFLECTING ON THE MEANING

The apostle Paul had spent much of his life following the Jewish practices to the letter of the law. So he understood firsthand that just seeking to live up to the standards of the law had no power to save. Instead, he found salvation by placing his faith in Christ and that work that Jesus had done for his sake on the cross. He wanted all believers to experience this same freedom, and in this section of Colossians, he spells out how this can be accomplished.

First, recognize that your former sins have been buried in Christ. Paul writes, "[You were] buried with Him in baptism [and] also were raised with Him through faith in the working of God, who raised Him from the dead" (Colossians 2:12). When you put your faith in Christ and received His forgiveness, the Lord blotted out your past sins. It is as if they no longer exist! Now, instead of a set of *rules* to follow, you have a *relationship* with your heavenly Father. This relationship will naturally create in you a desire to follow Jesus' example and live in a way that honors Him. You have no illusions about earning your salvation through good works but understand you are saved only because of God's infinite grace and mercy.

Second, embrace the new life that Christ offers. Paul states, "[Jesus] has made [you] alive together with Him, having forgiven you all trespasses, having wiped out the handwriting of requirements that was against us, which was contrary to us" (verses. 13–14). Jesus has *wiped out* the require- ments of constantly striving to live up to the standards of the law. He knows that such a pursuit will only leave you defeated. Instead, He offers forgiveness when you fail. He gives you the opportunity to learn from mistakes, move on, and continue moving forward with your life in Christ.

Third, resist the temptation to judge others. Paul writes, "So let no one judge you in food or in drink, or regarding a festival or a new moon or sabbaths, which are a shadow of things to come" (verses 16–17). It is important for believers to hold one another to high standards of behav- ior—"As iron sharpens iron, so a man sharpens the countenance of his friend" (Proverbs 27:17). But it is never acceptable for us to sit in the place of God and judge others. Grace, love, and empathy should be the traits we demonstrate in our relationships. For those are the same traits that Christ has demonstrated to us.

Jesus came to free you from the burden of continually trying to live up to the standards of the law. He came to give you nothing less than *life*—and he wants you to experience that life "more abundantly" (John 10:10). Your part is to embrace that new life that Jesus offers.

JOURNALING YOUR RESPONSE

How have you been tempted in the past to earn favor with God by your actions? How will you combat that kind of temptation going forward?

LESSON *six*

STAY CENTERED

Colossians 3:1–11

GETTING STARTED

What are some ways you stay centered on a task when you are confronted with distractions?

_____

_____

_____

_____

_____

_____

_____

_____

_____

_____

_____

_____

SETTING THE STAGE

The apostle Paul has just concluded his arguments against the Judaizers who were attempting to place the Colossian Christians under the restrictions of the Old Testament law. Paul is clear that the believers have received freedom in Christ and are not bound by former customs such as circumcision and dietary restrictions. However, this does not mean they are free to do whatever they please. Rather, they must put to death their old selves.

As Paul moves into this next section of his letter, he sets forth what is required of the Colossian believers when it comes to their attitudes and actions. As he writes, "If then you were raised with Christ, seek those things which are above, where Christ is" (3:2). Once again, his words are likely a rebuke of the false teachers who had infiltrated their midst. The exact nature of their teaching is again not clear, but they seem to have been encouraging the Colossians to focus on temporal, earthly things. Paul wants them to aim higher in their thoughts.

Today, we receive all kinds of instructions on how we should live. Psychologists tell us we should look within for the answers. Opportunists tell us we should look around for opportunities. Optimists tell us we should look ahead. Pessimists say we should look out. But God says we should look *up*. We must seek a perspective that can come only from God, remembering, as Paul wrote to the church in Philippi, "Our citizenship is in heaven, from which we also eagerly wait for the Savior" (Philippians 3:20).

Paul is not suggesting that we become oblivious to the fact that we live on planet earth. We have to deal with earthly things every day. But we should not get so caught up in the daily worries of life that we lose our focus on Christ. We are residents of earth, but our citizenship is in heaven. So let's continually seek to keep our hearts and mind centered on heavenly things.

EXPLORING THE TEXT

Not Carnality but Christ (Colossians 3:1–5)

> ¹ If then you were raised with Christ, seek those things which are
> above, where Christ is, sitting at the right hand of God. ² Set your
> mind on things above, not on things on the earth. ³ For you died,

and your life is hidden with Christ in God. ⁴ When Christ who is our life appears, then you also will appear with Him in glory.

⁵ Therefore put to death your members which are on the earth: fornication, uncleanness, passion, evil desire, and covetousness, which is idolatry.

---

1. In this passage, Paul points out that believers have been "raised with Christ" (verse 1). Although we have not been raised from the dead in the same way that Jesus bodily rose from the dead, those of us who have placed our trust in Jesus have been raised from *spiritual* death to life in Christ. How does Paul say we should live as a result of our new life in Christ (see verses 1–3; see also Romans 12:2 and Philippians 4:8)?

_____

_____

_____

_____

_____

2. Paul calls the Colossian believers' attention to their sinful habits and thoughts—many of which were common and acceptable practices in Colossae at that time. Likewise, even though we have been raised with Christ, we still need to combat our evil tendencies while we live in our earthly bodies. What must we do to stay centered on Christ? From what things must we actively and intentionally turn away (see verse 5)?

_____

_____

_____

_____

_____

_____

Christ Is All and in All (Colossians 3:6–11)

⁶ Because of these things the wrath of God is coming upon the sons of disobedience, ⁷ in which you yourselves once walked when you lived in them.

⁸ But now you yourselves are to put off all these: anger, wrath, malice, blasphemy, filthy language out of your mouth. ⁹ Do not lie to one another, since you have put off the old man with his deeds, ¹⁰ and have put on the new man who is renewed in knowledge according to the image of Him who created him, ¹¹ where there is neither Greek nor Jew, circumcised nor uncircumcised, barbarian, Scythian, slave nor free, but Christ is all and in all.

3. Paul points out to the Colossians that before their conversion, they had been characterized by sinful and destructive behaviors. But now, as followers of Jesus, they are called to set aside every sinful behavior and "walk in newness of life" (Romans 6:4). What should characterize a person who is new in Christ (see Colossians 3:8–10)?

4. The world is riddled with prejudice between groups of people. But being renewed in Christ changes our perception of others, because Jesus Himself becomes the focus rather than the distinctions between people that cause divisions. What are some of the irrelevant divisions that often keep people from recognizing we are all one in Christ (see verse 11)?

_____

_____

_____

_____

_____

_____

_____

_____

_____

_____

GOING DEEPER

The apostle Paul frequently stressed the need for believers to put aside their old ways of life and embrace the new life that Jesus had given to them. Paul understood this would require them to be _transformed_ in their thinking as they purposefully chose to focus on the things of God. In his letter to the Romans, he explains this will require them to reject the ways of the world, seek the path of humility and self-sacrifice, and willingly be a servant to others.

Transformed by Christ (Romans 12:1–8)

> [1] I beseech you therefore, brethren, by the mercies of God, that you present your bodies a living sacrifice, holy, acceptable to God, which is your reasonable service. [2] And do not be conformed to this

world, but be transformed by the renewing of your mind, that you may prove what is that good and acceptable and perfect will of God.

[3] For I say, through the grace given to me, to everyone who is among you, not to think of himself more highly than he ought to think, but to think soberly, as God has dealt to each one a measure of faith. [4] For as we have many members in one body, but all the members do not have the same function, [5] so we, being many, are one body in Christ, and individually members of one another. [6] Having then gifts differing according to the grace that is given to us, let us use them: if prophecy, let us prophesy in proportion to our faith; [7] or ministry, let us use it in our ministering; he who teaches, in teaching; [8] he who exhorts, in exhortation; he who gives, with liberality; he who leads, with diligence; he who shows mercy, with cheerfulness.

---

5. Paul outlines what believers in Christ are expected to do in response to the gospel. What must believers do instead of being conformed to this world (see verses 1–3)? How does this instruction compare to what Paul advised the believers in Colossae (see Colossians 3:1–5)?

_____

_____

_____

_____

_____

_____

_____

_____

_____

_____

_____

_____

6. Paul encourages the believers in Rome to embrace their God-given gifts and use them to serve the church (see Romans 12:3–8). How would this instruction have helped the believers to focus their hearts and minds on Christ rather than themselves?

_____

_____

_____

_____

_____

_____

_____

_____

Paul understood that believers in Christ were engaged in a battle against an enemy who wanted them to stay stuck in their past sins and bound to their former way of life. Other writers of the New Testament recognized this same tension in the churches where they ministered. In the following passage, Peter explains what he has witnessed regarding the enemy's tactics and how followers of Jesus can strike back against his attacks.

Submit to God, Resist the Devil (1 Peter 5:5–11)

⁵ Likewise you younger people, submit yourselves to your elders. Yes, all of you be submissive to one another, and be clothed with humility, for

> "God resists the proud,
> But gives grace to the humble."

⁶ Therefore humble yourselves under the mighty hand of God, that He may exalt you in due time, ⁷ casting all your care upon Him, for He cares for you.

⁸ Be sober, be vigilant; because your adversary the devil walks about like a roaring lion, seeking whom he may devour. ⁹ Resist him, steadfast in the faith, knowing that the same sufferings are experienced by your brotherhood in the world. ¹⁰ But may the God of all grace, who called us to His eternal glory by Christ Jesus, after you have suffered a while, perfect, establish, strengthen, and settle you. ¹¹ To Him be the glory and the dominion forever and ever. Amen.

7. The Old Testament often describes persecutors as predatory lions that are waiting for just the right moment to attack their prey (see Psalms 7:2; 10:8–10; Jeremiah 4:7; Ezekiel 19:6; Nahum 2:11–13). Here, Peter compares the devil to a ferocious lion. How does he recommend we respond when we face such a dangerous enemy (see 1 Peter 5:6–9)?

8. Peter wants us to understand we are not alone in our fight against the devil. As Christians, we can stand strong together in our common experiences of suffering. Ultimately, what will God do for those who persevere in resisting the enemy (see verses 9–11)?

REVIEWING THE STORY

Paul continues to challenge the false teachers who had infiltrated the Colossian church and encourages believers in Jesus to reject their teachings by setting their minds on things that are from heaven above. He implores the Colossians to reject their former sinful natures—putting aside anger, wrath, malice, blasphemy, filthy language—and to embrace their new nature in Christ. In doing so, they will pass their time wisely as they await Jesus' return.

9. What is the "above" that Paul tells us to set our minds on (Colossians 3:1)?

_____

_____

_____

_____

_____

_____

_____

_____

10. What can we expect to receive if we stay centered on Christ (see Colossians 3:4)?

_____

_____

_____

_____

_____

_____

_____

11. What will unbelievers face when Christ returns
(see Colossians 3:6)?

_____

_____

_____

_____

_____

12. How does Paul describe the "new man" that we are to put on in
order to stay centered on Christ (Colossians 3:10)?

_____

_____

_____

_____

APPLYING THE MESSAGE

13. What "things of earth" are making it difficult for you to stay
centered on Christ?

_____

_____

_____

_____

_____

14. How can you rely on other believers as you embrace the new life
that God has for you?

_____

_____

_____

_____

_____

REFLECTING ON THE MEANING

In this section of Colossians, Paul encourages believers to keep their focus on Christ in the midst of the pressures and stress of this world. Now, you may be wondering how this is possible—how you go from being "earth-centered" to being "heaven-centered." The following are three suggestions to help you in your quest for Christ-centeredness.

First, seek God's will. Jesus said, "Seek first the kingdom of God and His righteousness, and all these things shall be added to you" (Matthew 6:33). People try to read that verse backward. But one person rephrased it well: "Take care of the things that are important to God, and He will take care of the things that are important to you."

Second, search God's Word. The story of Mary and Martha is instructive in this regard. As you will recall, Martha was the pro-active, Type-A personality who never saw a to-do list she didn't like. When Jesus came for a visit, Martha was consumed with busywork and actually got upset at Mary for not helping. Jesus' reply to Martha is one you can apply in your life: "Martha, Martha, you are worried and troubled about many things. But one thing is needed, and Mary has chosen that good part, which will not be taken away from her" (Luke 10:41–42). Mary understood that it was far more important to get to know Jesus better, and focus on His teaching, than to be a busybody consumed with preparations.

Third, support God's Work. The connection between your treasure and your heart is one that cannot be ignored. Jesus said not to accumulate material treasures here on earth but to lay up "treasures in heaven, where neither moth nor rust destroys . . . for where your treasure is, there your heart will be also" (Matthew 6:20–21). You could call that an investment manifesto for children of the kingdom. Pour yourself into eternal things—things that affect the invisible world and change the population of heaven. If you want to keep your heart centered on heavenly things, you must invest your treasure in heavenly things.

The more you give yourself to God's purposes, the more centered on Christ you will become. Insisting on biblical priorities, staying interested in

God's Word, and investing your treasure in heaven will keep you centered on Christ until He comes again.

JOURNALING YOUR RESPONSE

How are your current priorities helping you or hindering you in staying centered on Jesus?

PUTTING ON THE NEW MAN

Colossians 3:12–17

GETTING STARTED

Why do you think it is often so hard to break bad habits?

_____

_____

_____

_____

_____

_____

_____

_____

_____

_____

_____

_____

_____

SETTING THE STAGE

The apostle Paul began this section of his letter with an appeal for the Colossian believers to set their minds on things above rather than on things of this earth. They were to "put off the old man with his deeds" (Colossians 3:9). This meant putting to death vices such as fornication, uncleanness, evil desires, covetousness, wrath, malice, blasphemy, and lying.

Paul will now expound on this point, showing that believers in Christ are to not only *put off* the vices of the "old man" but also *put on* the virtues of the "new man" (verse 10). They are to demonstrate qualities such as "tender mercies, kindness, humility, meekness, longsuffering," "bearing with one another" and "forgiving one another" (verses 12–13). Above all, believers are to "put on love, which is the bond of perfection" (verse 14) as they allow "the peace of God" to rule in their hearts and "the word of Christ" to dwell in their minds (verses 15–16).

Paul did not call the Colossian believers to such a high standard because he saw something extraordinary in them. (Remember, he had never met them.) Nor did he call them to lead such exemplary lives due to any reports he had received of their inner fortitude. Rather, he called them to such a standard because he understood the *transforming power of Christ*. His encounter with the risen Christ on the road to Damascus had forever changed his life. He wanted the Colossians to witness that same transformation in their own lives.

EXPLORING THE TEXT

Character of the New Man (Colossians 3:12–14)

¹² Therefore, as the elect of God, holy and beloved, put on tender mercies, kindness, humility, meekness, longsuffering; ¹³ bearing with one another, and forgiving one another, if anyone has a complaint against another; even as Christ forgave you, so you also must do. ¹⁴ But above all these things put on love, which is the bond of perfection.

1. Paul has just noted the Colossians belong to a new humanity where "there is neither Greek nor Jew, circumcised nor uncircumcised" (verse 11). They have put their trust in Christ and are united by a common mission. How does Paul describe this new status? What are the characteristics that members of this new humanity exhibit (see verses 12–13)?

_____

_____

_____

_____

_____

_____

_____

_____

_____

2. Paul believed that Jesus' sacrificial death on the cross served as both the pattern and the motivation for love among believers. This was a love that motivated Jesus to say from the cross, "Father, forgive them, for they do not know what they do" (Luke 23:34). How does Paul call the believers to likewise forgive one another (see Colossians 3:13–14)?

_____

_____

_____

_____

_____

_____

_____

_____

_____

Do All in the Name of the Lord Jesus (Colossians 3:15–17)

¹⁵ And let the peace of God rule in your hearts, to which also you were called in one body; and be thankful. ¹⁶ Let the word of Christ dwell in you richly in all wisdom, teaching and admonishing one another in psalms and hymns and spiritual songs, singing with grace in your hearts to the Lord. ¹⁷ And whatever you do in word or deed, do all in the name of the Lord Jesus, giving thanks to God the Father through Him.

3. Paul had noted in his letter to the Romans that the kingdom of God is characterized by "righteousness and peace and joy in the Holy Spirit" (14:17). Here, he calls the Colossians to allow God's peace to rule in their hearts as they work together as one body. How could they develop such peace and joy within the body of Christ (see Colossians 3:15–16)?

4. Paul states the believers are to conduct their worship with teaching, admonishing, and singing (see verse 16). These are *outward* actions that should reflect the *inward* attitude of our hearts. When we put on the "new man," what should be our guiding principle in not just our worship but also in *everything* we say and do (see verse 17)?

_____

_____

_____

_____

_____

_____

_____

_____

_____

_____

Going Deeper

Paul understood the challenges of putting on the "new man." As he was quick to confess, his own struggles with putting on the new man were internal as well as external. In the following portion of his letter to the believers in Rome, he was especially candid about the battle that was raging inside him between the old and new man.

The Law Cannot Save (Romans 7:13–17)

13 Has then what is good become death to me? Certainly not! But sin, that it might appear sin, was producing death in me through what is good, so that sin through the commandment might become exceedingly sinful. 14 For we know that the law is spiritual, but I am carnal, sold under sin. 15 For what I am doing, I do not understand.

For what I will to do, that I do not practice; but what I hate, that I do. ¹⁶ If, then, I do what I will not to do, I agree with the law that it is good. ¹⁷ But now, it is no longer I who do it, but sin that dwells in me.

---

5. God created us in His image, and because of this we have within us the desire to do good. However, because of the Fall, our sinful nature creates in us the desire to sin—not just once, but again and again throughout our lives. What does Paul say that this inherent desire within us produces? What are the results of operating in the "old man" (see verse 13)?

_____

_____

_____

_____

_____

_____

_____

_____

_____

6. How does Paul describe this battle raging inside him between the old and new man? What does he indicate is the source of the problem (see verses 14–17)?

_____

_____

_____

_____

_____

_____

_____

_____

A Wretched State (Romans 7:18–25)

[18] For I know that in me (that is, in my flesh) nothing good dwells; for to will is present with me, but how to perform what is good I do not find. [19] For the good that I will to do, I do not do; but the evil I will not to do, that I practice. [20] Now if I do what I will not to do, it is no longer I who do it, but sin that dwells in me.

[21] I find then a law, that evil is present with me, the one who wills to do good. [22] For I delight in the law of God according to the inward man. [23] But I see another law in my members, warring against the law of my mind, and bringing me into captivity to the law of sin which is in my members. [24] O wretched man that I am! Who will deliver me from this body of death? [25] I thank God—through Jesus Christ our Lord!

So then, with the mind I myself serve the law of God, but with the flesh the law of sin.

7. What does Paul mean when he says that "nothing good" dwells within him? What results has he seen in his life that proves this is true (see verses 18–20)?

8. Paul describes a tension we all experience—the struggle between *wanting* to do what is right and actually *doing* what is right (see verses 21–23). It is a condition that leads him to exclaim, "Who will deliver me from this body of death?" (verse 24)? How does Paul answer his own question (see verse 25)?

_____

_____

_____

_____

_____

_____

REVIEWING THE STORY

Paul instructs the believers in Corinth to let their actions and attitudes reflect their new status in Christ. Qualities such as kindness and mercy should draw people to them and give them opportunities to share their faith. What is more, the virtues of the new man will serve a valuable role in their congregation. Their shared commitment to long-suffering, empathy, loving confrontation, forgiveness, and peace is essential to the lifeblood of their church.

9. Why are the Colossian believers expected to put on the qualities of the new man (see Colossians 3:12)?

_____

_____

_____

_____

_____

10. What characteristic of the new man does Paul single out over all the others (see Colossians 3:14)?

11. What does Paul urge the Colossian believers to do in light of the fact they are "called in one body" (Colossians 3:15)?

12. When believers in Christ put on the new man, what should be their attitude toward God the Father (see Colossians 3:17)?

APPLYING THE MESSAGE

13. How would you describe the battle that rages inside of you between the old man and the new man? How do you relate to Paul's words regarding his struggle?

_____

_____

_____

_____

_____

14. What characteristics of the new man do you most want people to see in you? Why?

_____

_____

_____

_____

_____

REFLECTING ON THE MEANING

In this section of Colossians, Paul instructs us to "put on" the character of the new man (Colossians 3:12). But the reality is that putting on this character of the new man can prove to be quite a challenge. It won't always feel comfortable on us. Why? Because we have been putting on the character of the old man for so long that we have grown accustomed to it. Fortunately, there are certain steps that we can take to help facilitate the process.

First, we can draw on the peace of God. Paul instructs us to "let the peace of God" rule in our hearts (verse 15). It is easy to give in to our emotions during times of conflict and stress and lash out in anger, wrath, or malice. These vices can be formidable opponents, for just when we think we have them under control, they come roaring back with a vengeance. So we need to make it a practice to turn to the Holy Spirit when we feel these emotions rising up within us. We *can* allow the peace of God to rule in our hearts. As we do, we will learn and grow from each battle as the Holy Spirit gives us the victory over our vices.

Second, we can spend time in the Word of God. Paul states that we must "let the word of Christ" dwell within us (verse 16). We find wisdom in the pages of God's Word for incorporating the virtues of the new man in our lives. We find role models who show us what those virtues look like in action. We find cautionary tales of what happens when those virtues are neglected. We receive instruction and encouragement for living as God wants us to live.

Third, we can surround ourselves with fellow workers. Paul writes that we are to be "teaching and admonishing one another" (verse 16). The word *teaching* implies that we are to listen to one another, learn from one another, and build up one another in the faith. The term *admonishing* implies that we are to confront one another in love when we recognize a sinful pattern of behavior. The Christian life was never meant to be led in isolation. God established the body of Christ so that we could run the race that He has set for us and not falter.

Fourth, we can maintain an attitude of thanksgiving. Paul concludes by instructing us to do all things "in the name of the Lord Jesus, giving thanks to God the Father" (verse 17). It is easy to get discouraged as we seek to put on the new man. Failures and setbacks may lead to us believing that we will never change and embrace the new virtues that God has for us. At such times, we need to remember all that God has done in the past . . . and recognize just how far He has taken us in the present. As we do this, we will find ourselves praising Him for what He has done and discovering the strength to press on into the future.

Experts say that it takes about sixty-six days for a behavior to become a habit. So ask God to make you aware of opportunities to *practice* putting on the virtues of the new man. In time, the virtues of the new man will become—appropriately enough—second nature to you.

JOURNALING YOUR RESPONSE

What "new man" practice can you start today that will ultimately develop into a habit? How will you begin to put this practice into effect in your life?

FULLY ENGAGED

Colossians 3:18–25

GETTING STARTED

What tends to motivate you to put your whole heart and mind into an activity?

_____

_____

_____

_____

_____

_____

_____

_____

_____

_____

_____

_____

_____

_____

_____

_____

_____

_____

_____

SETTING THE STAGE

If you have ever driven a car with a stick shift, you are familiar with the clutch. Technically speaking, it is the instrument used to disengage the car's engine from the drive train or gearbox. When the clutch pedal is pushed to the floor, and the engine is disengaged, the gears can be shifted. When the clutch is released and returned to its normal position, the drivetrain is reengaged, and the power of the engine causes the automobile to move.

There are supposed to be only two positions for a clutch: engaged or disengaged. People who try to "ride the clutch" in the middle ground will burn it out . . . and there is a special aroma that goes along with burned-out clutches! With this image in mind, we come to these closing words from Paul in this section of Colossians: "Whatever you do, do it heartily, as to the Lord and not to men, knowing that from the Lord you will receive the reward of the inheritance; for you serve the Lord Christ" (Colossians 3:23–24).

The apostle is referring here to a fully engaged life in all of our relationships—including our spouses, our children, and those in our community. It is the type of life in which we are not merely "riding the clutch" in the choices that we make. It is a kind of life not as concerned with achieving success, or gaining satisfaction, or finding enjoyment in this life, but with an honest desire to make a difference for Christ in this world. It is a kind of life where we may find ourselves out of our comfort zone—and sometimes *far* outside of our comfort zone.

This is the kind of life where we live for Christ with nothing held back. We do whatever He asks when He asks us to do it. And as we do, we find that we can look back with no regrets.

EXPLORING THE TEXT

The Christian Home (Colossians 3:18–21)

18 Wives, submit to your own husbands, as is fitting in the Lord.

19 Husbands, love your wives and do not be bitter toward them.

²⁰ Children, obey your parents in all things, for this is well pleasing to the Lord.

²¹ Fathers, do not provoke your children, lest they become discouraged.

---

1. Paul here offers guidance to families as to how they can honor Jesus in the way they relate to one another. What are his instructions for wives and husbands (see verses 18–19)?

_____

_____

_____

_____

_____

2. What are Paul's instructions for children and "fathers" or parents (see verses 20–21)? How do these qualities relate to what Paul has just discussed about how the "elect of God" (verse 12) should interact with one another?

_____

_____

_____

_____

_____

_____

Do It Heartily, As to the Lord (Colossians 3:22–25)

²² Bondservants, obey in all things your masters according to the flesh, not with eyeservice, as men-pleasers, but in sincerity of heart, fearing God. ²³ And whatever you do, do it heartily, as to the Lord and not to men, ²⁴ knowing that from the Lord you will receive the reward of the inheritance; for you serve the Lord Christ. ²⁵ But he

who does wrong will be repaid for what he has done, and there is no partiality.

---

3. In the first-century world of Paul's day, slavery was practiced not based on race but as a way for people to pay off debt. While Paul does not condone the practice of slavery in his teaching, he does instruct slaves (bondservants) and masters to develop integrity and mutual respect for one another within their relationships. How does Paul instruct slaves to engage both in their work and with their masters (see verses 22–23)?

_____

_____

_____

_____

4. Paul's instructions to slaves applies to anyone who works for another person. Our motivation for being wholeheartedly engaged in our work and responsibilities should be fueled by a desire to honor the Lord, not any earthly employer. What reason does Paul offer for why we are ultimately working for the Lord and not people (see verse 24)?

_____

_____

_____

_____

GOING DEEPER

Other writers of Scripture also recognized the importance of being completely committed to God. King David stands out as an example of "a man after [God's] own heart" (1 Samuel 13:14) who held nothing back in his worship and service to God. In the following psalm, he encourages us to follow this same course and points out the benefits that we will receive as we do.

The Heritage of the Righteous (Psalm 37:3–8)

³ Trust in the LORD, and do good;
Dwell in the land, and feed on His faithfulness.
⁴ Delight yourself also in the LORD,
And He shall give you the desires of your heart.

⁵ Commit your way to the LORD,
Trust also in Him,
And He shall bring it to pass.
⁶ He shall bring forth your righteousness as the light,
And your justice as the noonday.

⁷ Rest in the LORD, and wait patiently for Him;
Do not fret because of him who prospers in his way,
Because of the man who brings wicked schemes to pass.
⁸ Cease from anger, and forsake wrath;
Do not fret—it only causes harm.

5. What does David say will happen when we choose to trust in the Lord, feed on His faithfulness, delight ourselves in Him, and commit our ways to Him (see verses 3–6)?

_____

_____

_____

_____

_____

_____

6. God offers a promise of rest when we commit to completely following His ways. What kind of rest does He provide? What *don't* we have to worry about (see verses 7–8)?

_____

_____

_____

_____

The Steps of a Good Man (Psalm 37:23–29)

²³ The steps of a good man are ordered by the LORD,
And He delights in his way.
²⁴ Though he fall, he shall not be utterly cast down;
For the LORD upholds him with His hand.

²⁵ I have been young, and now am old;
Yet I have not seen the righteous forsaken,
Nor his descendants begging bread.
²⁶ He is ever merciful, and lends;
And his descendants are blessed.

²⁷ Depart from evil, and do good;
And dwell forevermore.
²⁸ For the LORD loves justice,
And does not forsake His saints;
They are preserved forever,
But the descendants of the wicked shall be cut off.
²⁹ The righteous shall inherit the land,
And dwell in it forever.

7. David states that the Lord orders the steps of those who trust in Him and choose to follow His ways. What happens when a "good man" falls?

What promise is given in these verses for those who seek the path of righteousness (see verses 23–26)?

_____

_____

_____

_____

8. David urges followers of God to "depart from evil" (verse 27). What happens to those who refuse to leave behind the former sinful ways of their past (see verses 28–29)?

_____

_____

_____

_____

REVIEWING THE STORY

Paul identifies the traits of a family fully engaged in bringing honor to the Lord through their relationships: a wife submitting to her husband, a husband demonstrating sacrificial love for his wife, children obeying their parents, and a father being careful not to provoke his children. Paul also emphasizes the importance of God-fearing obedience, even beyond the family. He helps the Colossian believers recognize that those who live a life centered on Christ will be rewarded and those who choose a less-engaged alternative will suffer the consequences.

9. What two instructions does the apostle Paul offer to husbands (see Colossians 3:19)?

_____

_____

_____

_____

10. What happens when fathers provoke their children
(see Colossians 3:21)?

_____

_____

_____

_____

11. What knowledge encourages us to do things heartily as to the Lord
(see Colossians 3:23–24)?

_____

_____

_____

_____

12. What happens when we choose not to do something heartily as to
the Lord (see Colossians 3:25)?

_____

_____

_____

_____

APPLYING THE MESSAGE

13. What are some ways that you can show love today in your family
relationships?

_____

_____

_____

_____

14. What does it look like for you to lead an engaged life for Christ? What needs to happen for you to engage more in the opportunities you have been given?

REFLECTING ON THE MEANING

In Colossians 3:23–24, Paul instructs us on how to fully engage in serving Christ in our families and other relationships. There are four important points to recognize in Paul's words.

First, we are to serve God in "whatever" we do. The word *whatever* covers a vast territory of activity. Paul makes no distinctions between the pleasant and the unpleasant. We are to dive into *all* our tasks with full and equal engagement. This includes fixing a leaky faucet, changing diapers, paying bills, and resolving conflicts between kids.

Second, we are to serve God "heartily." To do something "heartily" means that we do it with all our being—with all that we are. As David writes, "Bless the LORD, O my soul; and all that is within me, bless His holy name!" (Psalm 103:1). The Lord doesn't want us to serve Him or worship Him *half*heartedly. He wants us to do it with all that is within us.

Third, we are to serve others "as to the Lord." This is the great secret: as we love and serve others, we are actually loving and serving God. One of the beautiful things about serving God is that we only have one boss—one person to please. As Paul wrote, "For none of us lives to himself, and no one dies to himself. For if we live, we live to the Lord; and if we die, we die to the Lord. Therefore, whether we live or die, we are the Lord's" (Romans 14:7–8).

Fourth, we are to serve out of God's strength. Paul writes, [Know] that from the Lord you will receive the reward . . . for you serve the Lord Christ" (Colossians 3:24). The source of a fully engaged life is *God*. We can love and serve others not because people are inherently lovable—in fact, the opposite is usually true. But we can love and serve them anyway because the source of our love is God. As John wrote, "We love . . . because He first loved us" (1 John 4:19).

JOURNALING YOUR RESPONSE

What are some areas in which you sense God is urging you to serve Him more heartily in those things that He has called you to do? How will you act on that urging from the Lord?

_____

_____

_____

_____

_____

_____

_____

_____

_____

_____

_____

_____

_____

_____

_____

_____

_____

_____

THE HOLY SPIRIT'S WORK

Colossians 4:1–9

GETTING STARTED

What are some of the traits of a person who is led by the Holy Spirit?

_____

_____

_____

_____

_____

_____

_____

_____

_____

_____

_____

_____

_____

SETTING THE STAGE

Charles Proteus Steinmetz was gifted with an extraordinary scientific mind. He built the generators that powered Henry Ford's first automobile plant. One day, those generators broke down, and the plant came to a halt. The plant manager brought in repairmen to fix the problem, but none of them could get the generators going again.

So Henry Ford called in Charlie to tackle the problem. The genius came in and spent the first day and night listening to the generators and scribbling computations in his notebook. On the second night, he asked for a ladder, climbed up to one generator, and made a chalk mark on the side. He instructed the workers to remove a plate at the mark and replace sixteen windings from the field core. They did, and the problem was solved.

Henry Ford was thrilled with the outcome . . . until he received an invoice for Charlie's services in the amount of $10,000. Ford balked at the figure and asked for an itemized bill. Charlie responded personally with this explanation: "Making chalk mark on generator: $1. Knowing where to make the mark: $9,999." Ford paid the bill.

This story serves as a reminder of the Holy Spirit's work in our lives. When things go wrong, we can turn to any number of sources for a solution. But only the Holy Spirit knows where to make the right "mark" in our lives. As we allow Him to do His work within us, He will get our "generators" moving again so we can accomplish His purposes in the world.

In this closing chapter of Colossians, Paul offers a wonderful description of what it looks like when the Holy Spirit is in control in our lives. As Paul notes, in particular we will notice how the Holy Spirit transforms our *worship*, our *testimony* to the world, and the *words* that we speak to others. Paul also reminds us that the Holy Spirit is available to us any time. If we trust Him and stay obedient to His control, we will lead victorious lives for Christ.

EXPLORING THE TEXT

A Call to Prayer (Colossians 4:1–4)

---

⁴ Masters, give your bondservants what is just and fair, knowing that you also have a Master in heaven.

² Continue earnestly in prayer, being vigilant in it with thanksgiving; ³ meanwhile praying also for us, that God would open to us a door for the word, to speak the mystery of Christ, for which I am also in chains, ⁴ that I may make it manifest, as I ought to speak.

1. Believers must be vigilant in prayer by not only paying attention to what God is doing in their lives but also by watching out for what the forces of evil are doing (see 1 Peter 5:8). Along with vigilance, what other characteristics are vital to prayer (see Colossians 4:2)?

_____

_____

_____

_____

2. Paul often asked in his letters for the churches to pray for him and his coworkers (see Romans 15:30–32; 2 Corinthians 1:11; 1 Thessalonians 5:25; 2 Thessalonians 3:1). What does Paul ask the Colossian believers to pray for here (see Colossians 4:3–4)?

_____

_____

_____

_____

Christian Graces (Colossians 4:5–9)

⁵ Walk in wisdom toward those who are outside, redeeming the time. ⁶ Let your speech always be with grace, seasoned with salt, that you may know how you ought to answer each one.

⁷ Tychicus, a beloved brother, faithful minister, and fellow servant in the Lord, will tell you all the news about me. ⁸ I am sending him

to you for this very purpose, that he may know your circumstances and comfort your hearts, [9] with Onesimus, a faithful and beloved brother, who is one of you. They will make known to you all things which are happening here.

3. Paul recognized the Christian life is not lived in a vacuum—believers interact with non-believers all the time. Paul wanted the Colossians—and all followers of Christ—to consider how their actions influence those around them. What Spirit-led principles does Paul say should guide the Colossian believers' interactions with unbelievers (see verses 5–6)?

4. The identity of Tychicus remains a mystery, though many Bible scholars believe he is the person Paul describes in Ephesians 6:21 as "a beloved brother and faithful minister in the Lord" (see also Acts 20:4; 2 Timothy 4:12; Titus 3:12). Onesimus is believed to be the slave of Philemon (see Philemon 1:10). What evidence do we see of the Holy Spirit's guidance in the lives of Tychicus and Onesimus (see verses 7–9)?

GOING DEEPER

The apostle Paul had witnessed the transforming power of the Holy Spirit in his own life, and he wanted all believers in Christ to receive the same. This was a power that had first been promised by Jesus to His disciples. In the following accounts from John, we see how Christ revealed the coming of the Holy Spirit and some of the work He would do in their lives.

Jesus Promises Another Helper (John 14:15–21)

15 "If you love Me, keep My commandments. 16 And I will pray the Father, and He will give you another Helper, that He may abide with you forever—17 the Spirit of truth, whom the world cannot receive, because it neither sees Him nor knows Him; but you know Him, for He dwells with you and will be in you. 18 I will not leave you orphans; I will come to you.

19 "A little while longer and the world will see Me no more, but you will see Me. Because I live, you will live also. 20 At that day you will know that I am in My Father, and you in Me, and I in you. 21 He who has My commandments and keeps them, it is he who loves Me. And he who loves Me will be loved by My Father, and I will love him and manifest Myself to him."

5. Paul wrote to the Corinthians, "The natural man does not receive the things of the Spirit of God, for they are foolishness to him; nor can he know them, because they are spiritually discerned" (1 Corinthians 2:14). Why are unbelievers unable to recognize the activity of the Holy Spirit in the world (see John 14:15–17)?

_____

_____

_____

_____

6. How does Jesus describe the Holy Spirit in this passage? What did Jesus say would happen after He left this world and the Holy Spirit came upon His disciples (see verses 17–21)?

The Gift of Peace (John 14:25–28)

25 "These things I have spoken to you while being present with you. 26 But the Helper, the Holy Spirit, whom the Father will send in My name, He will teach you all things, and bring to your remembrance all things that I said to you. 27 Peace I leave with you, My peace I give to you; not as the world gives do I give to you. Let not your heart be troubled, neither let it be afraid. 28 You have heard Me say to you, 'I am going away and coming back to you.' If you loved Me, you would rejoice because I said, 'I am going to the Father,' for My Father is greater than I.

---

7. What further benefits does Jesus say the Holy Spirit will bring (see verses 25–26)?

---

8. Jesus reassured His followers that they would not be left on their own in this world and that His Spirit would carry out His work in them. Why did Jesus say the disciples could actually *rejoice* that He was going to be leaving them (see verse 28)?

_____

_____

_____

_____

REVIEWING THE STORY

Paul's final words to the Colossians reflect on the Holy Spirit's control of their lives. He urges them to allow the Holy Spirit to guide them in the way they treat those who are "below" them socially, in the way they pray, in the way they conduct themselves as believers, and in the way they share and defend their faith. Paul states that he is sending his coworkers Tychicus and Onesimus to Colossae to relate all the news about him and to provide comfort to them.

9. What did Paul want the Colossian believers to pray for on his behalf (see Colossians 4:3)?

_____

_____

_____

_____

10. What minor inconvenience did Paul endure in allowing the Holy Spirit to control his life (see Colossians 4:3)?

_____

_____

_____

_____

11. What should be our attitude and approach toward unbelievers (see Colossians 4:5–6)?

_____

_____

_____

_____

_____

_____

_____

12. For what tasks did the Holy Spirit equip and prepare Tychicus and Onesimus (see Colossians 4:8–9)?

_____

_____

_____

_____

_____

_____

APPLYING THE MESSAGE

13. What areas of your life are most in need of the Holy Spirit's control right now?

_____

_____

_____

_____

_____

_____

_____

14. What steps can you take to surrender control to the Holy Spirit in those areas?

_____

_____

_____

_____

REFLECTING ON THE MEANING

In the final chapter of Colossians, Paul urges us to pursue righteousness and conduct ourselves in such a way that others will see there is something different about us. We do this in the example we set in our worship, our walk, and our witness. Let's look at each of these points.

First, we set an example in the way we worship. Paul instructs us to pray earnestly, vigilantly, and with thanksgiving (see verse 2). We don't go into a time of worship haphazardly but fully devote our attention to God—remaining mentally alert and spiritually awake. We make it a point to express our thanksgiving to God for His acts of mercy in our lives.

Second, we set an example in the way we walk with God. Paul instructs us to "walk in wisdom" (verse 5), which means to walk carefully. People outside the church are watching us closely, looking for anything that might disqualify our message, so we need to allow the Holy Spirit to work in us so we will walk in a wise manner. Unbelievers should be able to look at way we conduct our affairs and also be drawn to the Source of the wisdom that dwells within us.

Third, we set an example in our witness. Paul instructs us to let our "speech always be with grace" and "seasoned with salt" (verse 6). We must become comfortable in sharing our faith—our testimony of grace—with anyone, at any time, and in any place. As we do, our words should be compelling ("seasoned with salt") so that people will *thirst* for what we have to say about Christ. We share what God has done for us and how He has transformed our lives.

As we set an example in our worship, our walk, and our witness, we preach the message the world needs to "hear." When we do, God uses our lives to draw others into His family.

JOURNALING YOUR RESPONSE

How can you tell if the Holy Spirit is controlling your worship, your walk, and your witness?

PRAISE FOR FELLOW WORKERS

Colossians 4:10–18

GETTING STARTED

Who are your fellow workers in the faith? What are some of the ways they have helped you?

_____

_____

_____

_____

_____

_____

_____

_____

_____

_____

_____

_____

_____

_____

_____

_____

_____

_____

_____

SETTING THE STAGE

Paul ends his letter to the Colossians by identifying some of the people who are with him in his ministry. He calls them beloved brothers, faithful ministers, and fellow workers for the Lord (see Colossians 4:7, 9, 11). Some of the names that Paul mentions are familiar to us, while others are found nowhere else in the Bible. Regardless, the work of each of these individuals is forever linked with the work of Christ, simply because Paul made the effort to mention them.

The way Paul refers to his fellow workers speaks to his humility. He seems intent on demonstrating to the Colossians that his ministry was not a one-man show—that he was not the only one in chains for the sake of the gospel. Yet Paul's final greetings involve more than just giving credit where credit was due. Paul also wanted the Colossians to know that a person like Epaphras was working diligently on their behalf. He wanted them to understand that in the body of Christ, people use their gifts for the benefit of the entire body. He wanted them to understand that every spiritual gift and ability—whether it is evangelism, teaching or, in the case of Epaphras, communication and prayer—is essential to the life of the church.

Paul spent so much of his time warning against false teachers and the damage they had caused that he must have relished the opportunity to name some genuine workers for Christ. Throughout this final portion of his letter, you can sense his affection and gratitude for the people he lists. These are the people who refreshed Paul and brought him joy.

EXPLORING THE TEXT

Paul's Fellow Workers (Colossians 4:10–13)

---

[10] Aristarchus my fellow prisoner greets you, with Mark the cousin of Barnabas (about whom you received instructions: if he comes to you, welcome him), [11] and Jesus who is called Justus. These

are my only fellow workers for the kingdom of God who are of the circumcision; they have proved to be a comfort to me.

¹² Epaphras, who is one of you, a bondservant of Christ, greets you, always laboring fervently for you in prayers, that you may stand perfect and complete in all the will of God. ¹³ For I bear him witness that he has a great zeal for you, and those who are in Laodicea, and those in Hierapolis.

---

1. When Paul wrote Colossians, it is possible that Aristarchus was with him in prison in Rome (see Acts 27:2). Mark refers to John Mark, who accompanied Peter in his ministry (see 1 Peter 5:13) and authored the Gospel of Mark. Justus is an unknown early believer (he is mentioned in Acts 1:23 and 18:7). Why do you think the companionship and support of Aristarchus, Mark, and Justus was so meaningful to Paul (see Colossians 4:10–11)?

2. Paul previously described Epaphras as a "dear fellow servant" and a "faithful minister of Christ" (Colossians 1:7–8). Epaphras faithfully brought the gospel to the Colossians and served as a teacher in the Colossian church. Here Paul greets the Colossians on behalf of Epaphras. What did Paul want the believers to know about Epaphras (see verses 12–13)?

_____

_____

_____

_____

_____

_____

_____

_____

_____

_____

_____

_____

Closing Exhortations and Blessing (Colossians 4:14–18)

14 Luke the beloved physician and Demas greet you. 15 Greet the brethren who are in Laodicea, and Nymphas and the church that is in his house.

16 Now when this epistle is read among you, see that it is read also in the church of the Laodiceans, and that you likewise read the epistle from Laodicea. 17 And say to Archippus, "Take heed to the ministry which you have received in the Lord, that you may fulfill it."

18 This salutation by my own hand—Paul. Remember my chains. Grace be with you. Amen.

3. Paul concludes by mentioning Luke and Damas, who are also included at the end of Paul's letter to Philemon (see Philemon 1:24). He then mentions the believers in Laodicea, a city about ten miles from Colossae. What instructions does Paul give to the believers in Colossae that would encourage fellowship among churches (see Colossians 4:16)?

_____

_____

_____

_____

4. Paul often dictated his letters through a scribe or a secretary. For example, we know that a man named Tertius wrote the letter to the Romans on behalf of Paul (see Romans 16:22). But here, Paul makes a point to tell his Colossian readers that he wrote the salutation to them himself. What does Paul want the Colossian believers to keep in mind about him (see Colossians 4:18)?

_____

_____

_____

_____

GOING DEEPER

The fact that Paul mentions Mark (also called John Mark), even in passing, is a testament to the healing nature of forgiveness and the power of second chances. Mark was the nephew of Barnabas, one of Paul's traveling companions. Barnabas had arranged for his nephew to accompany him and Paul on their first missionary journey, but John Mark abandoned them and returned to Jerusalem (see Acts 13:13). Later, when Paul and Barnabas were planning a second journey, Barnabas wanted to again bring his nephew. However, John Mark's departure had left such a bad impression on Paul that he refused, and the two ultimately parted ways.

Division Over John Mark (Acts 15:36–41)

36 Then after some days Paul said to Barnabas, "Let us now go back and visit our brethren in every city where we have preached the word of the Lord, and see how they are doing." 37 Now Barnabas was determined to take with them John called Mark. 38 But Paul insisted that they should not take with them the one who had departed from them in Pamphylia, and had not gone with them to the work. 39 Then the contention became so sharp that they parted from one another. And so Barnabas took Mark and sailed to Cyprus; 40 but Paul chose Silas and departed, being commended by the brethren to the grace of God. 41 And he went through Syria and Cilicia, strengthening the churches.

5. Luke here describes a point of contention that drove a wedge not only between Paul and John Mark but also between Paul and Barnabas. Why did Paul refuse to take John Mark with him on his second missionary journey (see verses 36–38)?

6. Luke includes details in his writing that reveal the relational difficulties faced by those who were tasked with proclaiming the gospel in the first century. What happened as a result of Paul and Barnabas's disagreement over John Mark (verses 39–40)?

_____

_____

_____

_____

_____

_____

Paul also mentions John Mark in his second letter to Timothy, which provides further evidence that the two men ultimately reconciled. When this letter was written, the apostle was facing imminent death at the hands of the Roman authorities, and many of his friends had abandoned him. So Paul is intent on calling out those individuals who had been faithful in his ministry.

Calling Out the Faithful (2 Timothy 4:9–18)

⁹ Be diligent to come to me quickly; ¹⁰ for Demas has forsaken me, having loved this present world, and has departed for Thessalonica— Crescens for Galatia, Titus for Dalmatia. ¹¹ Only Luke is with me. Get Mark and bring him with you, for he is useful to me for ministry. ¹² And Tychicus I have sent to Ephesus. ¹³ Bring the cloak that I left with Carpus at Troas when you come—and the books, especially the parchments.

¹⁴ Alexander the coppersmith did me much harm. May the Lord repay him according to his works. ¹⁵ You also must beware of him, for he has greatly resisted our words.

¹⁶ At my first defense no one stood with me, but all forsook me. May it not be charged against them.

[17] But the Lord stood with me and strengthened me, so that the message might be preached fully through me, and that all the Gentiles might hear. Also I was delivered out of the mouth of the lion. [18] And the Lord will deliver me from every evil work and preserve me for His heavenly kingdom. To Him be glory forever and ever. Amen!

---

7. Paul notes that Demas and Alexander had forsaken him. Three other coworkers—Crescens, Titus, and Tychicus—had remained faithful but had departed to tend to other churches (see verses 9–15). How would you describe Paul's state of mind in this passage?

_____

_____

_____

_____

8. Why does Paul ask Timothy to bring John Mark with him when he comes (see verse 11)? What confidence does Paul have in spite of his difficulties (see verses 17–18)?

_____

_____

_____

_____

_____

REVIEWING THE STORY

Paul concludes his letter by sending greetings from his fellow workers. He wants the Colossians to know their names so they will welcome these men if they ever minister within the Colossian church. He singles out Epaphras for special mention to make the believers aware of how much he was doing on their behalf. Paul closes with an instruction for the Colossian church to share this letter with its sister congregation in Laodicea. He asks the Colossian believers to remember him in prayer, so that he might continue to minister in spite of his chains.

9. What circumstances did Aristarchus share in common with Paul (see Colossians 4:10)?

_____

_____

_____

_____

_____

_____

10. What was Epaphras's prayer for the Colossian believers (see Colossians 4:13)?

_____

_____

_____

_____

_____

_____

11. How does Paul refer to Luke (see Colossians 4:14)?

_____

_____

_____

_____

_____

_____

12. What was Paul's message to Archippus (see Colossians 4:17)?

_____

_____

_____

_____

_____

_____

APPLYING THE MESSAGE

13. Who are some of the people you would consider to be your "fellow workers in Christ"?

_____

_____

_____

_____

_____

_____

_____

14. How do you show your gratitude and appreciation for these fellow workers?

_____

_____

_____

_____

_____

_____

_____

REFLECTING ON THE MEANING

Paul makes a point in his letters to mention those individuals who helped shape the early church. One individual he calls out for special attention is Epaphras, whom he mentions at both the beginning and end of the letter (see 1:7–8; 4:12–13). As we read Paul's words, we can glean four takeaways from Epaphras's example on how to be a faithful minister of the gospel.

First, we must be persistent in our ministry. Paul refers to Epaphras as "a faithful minister of Christ" (1:7). It's one thing to minister during a moment of crisis or to rise to the occasion when the need arises. But it's something different to minister faithfully, year after year, in the same place. This is evidently what Epaphras did. His faithful and protracted ministry was observable and worthy of mention.

Second, we must be precise in our communication. In Colossians 1:8, Paul says that Epaphras "declared to us your love in the Spirit." Paul had never been to Colossae, so everything he knew about the Colossian believers came from Epaphras. His precise and detailed communication had allowed Paul to understand the need in Colossae and address it.

Third, we must be passionate in our prayers. In Colossians 4:12, Paul assures the Colossians that Epaphras was "always laboring fervently" in prayer on their behalf. His work can teach us something about our own prayer habits. We are to pray faithfully ("always"). Prayer isn't intended to be an occasional spiritual discipline. We are to pray fiercely ("laboring"). We must dedicate ourselves to prayer. We are also to pray "fervently." We must approach prayer with a passion—a zeal to spend time in God's presence on behalf of others.

Fourth, we must be particular about people. Paul writes that Epaphras had great zeal not only for the believers in Colossae but also for the believers in nearby Laodicea and Hierapolis (see 4:13). As believers, we can't pray fervently if we don't have a zeal and a love for people. When we love people, when we care deeply about people, and when we reach out to people, God will promote the prayer in our own lives for those people.

JOURNALING YOUR RESPONSE

Taking a cue from Epaphras, what changes can you make to recharge your prayer life?

MAKING AMENDS

Philemon 1:1–16

GETTING STARTED

What is the most difficult thing that you've had to do to make amends with someone?

_____

_____

_____

_____

_____

_____

_____

_____

_____

_____

_____

_____

_____

_____

SETTING THE STAGE

At first glance, Paul's letter to his friend Philemon seems to tell a rather straightforward story of betrayal, transformation, and making amends.

Philemon was a wealthy man in Colossae. The Colossian church met in his home. He and Paul had been acquainted for some time.

Onesimus was a more recent acquaintance of Paul who had proved his value by becoming a trusted friend and fellow worker. Paul had led both Philemon and Onesimus to Christ. But the two men shared another, more complicated connection. Onesimus was a runaway slave who had stolen from his master. Philemon *was* his master.

As previously noted, the practice of slavery was common in the Roman Empire. Many people, both inside and outside of the church, joined in this practice of owning slaves. Although some slaves were well treated, those who ran away could face the death penalty. It is for this reason that Paul writes to his old friend Philemon on behalf of his new friend Onesimus.

Paul's goal is to reconcile the two men. He urges Philemon to receive Onesimus as a Christian *brother*, not as a runaway slave deserving of punishment. In his delivery of the letter, Paul urges Onesimus to make amends with Philemon. According to the law of the land, Onesimus had an obligation to fulfill to Philemon. So Paul instructs Onesimus himself (along with Epaphras) to deliver the letter—and to begin making amends with Philemon.

This is the surface story—the narrative that informs Paul's letter to Philemon. However, a deeper study of the letter reveals a beautiful illustration of something much more profound.

EXPLORING THE TEXT

Greeting (Philemon 1:1–7)

---

[1] Paul, a prisoner of Christ Jesus, and Timothy our brother,

To Philemon our beloved friend and fellow laborer, [2] to the beloved Apphia, Archippus our fellow soldier, and to the church in your house:

[3] Grace to you and peace from God our Father and the Lord Jesus Christ.

⁴ I thank my God, making mention of you always in my prayers,
⁵ hearing of your love and faith which you have toward the Lord Jesus
and toward all the saints, ⁶ that the sharing of your faith may become
effective by the acknowledgment of every good thing which is in you
in Christ Jesus. ⁷ For we have great joy and consolation in your love,
because the hearts of the saints have been refreshed by you, brother.

---

1. Paul has confidence in Philemon's character and expresses his "great
joy and consolation" in Philemon's love for other believers (verse 7).
How had Philemon's reputation preceded him (see verses 5, 7)?

_____

_____

_____

_____

_____

_____

2. Paul employs his typical style (consistent with letter-writing in the
first century) of following his salutation with a statement of thanksgiving
for the recipient and then with a prayer for the recipient. What does Paul
pray for on behalf of Philemon (see verse 6)?

_____

_____

_____

_____

_____

_____

_____

The Plea for Onesimus (Philemon 1:8–16)

⁸ Therefore, though I might be very bold in Christ to command you what is fitting, ⁹ yet for love's sake I rather appeal to you—being such a one as Paul, the aged, and now also a prisoner of Jesus Christ—¹⁰ I appeal to you for my son Onesimus, whom I have begotten while in my chains, ¹¹ who once was unprofitable to you, but now is profitable to you and to me.

¹² I am sending him back. You therefore receive him, that is, my own heart, ¹³ whom I wished to keep with me, that on your behalf he might minister to me in my chains for the gospel. ¹⁴ But without your consent I wanted to do nothing, that your good deed might not be by compulsion, as it were, but voluntary.

¹⁵ For perhaps he departed for a while for this purpose, that you might receive him forever, ¹⁶ no longer as a slave but more than a slave—a beloved brother, especially to me but how much more to you, both in the flesh and in the Lord.

3. Paul knows that he is being "bold" in his letter to Philemon (verse 8), because he has no legal protection to offer Onesimus. He wants Onesimus to remain with him, yet he knows that Onesimus's fate rests solely in the hands and at the mercy of his master, Philemon. Why did Paul wish to keep Onesimus with him (see verses 12–14)?

4. Paul shows respect for Philemon's legal position as master while also showing respect for Onesimus's value—not as a slave to be owned but as a brother to be accepted. What does Paul want Philemon to know about Onesimus in this letter? What does Paul urge Philemon to consider regarding his treatment of Onesimus (see verses 10–12, 15–16)?

Going Deeper

Two issues at the heart of Paul's letter are *forgiveness* and *restoration*. Paul was asking Philemon to receive Onesimus back, forgive him for running away, and restore him in his household. Paul's words echo Jesus' words to His followers in the Sermon on the Mount. As the following passages relate, God desires all of His children to forgive one another and be reconciled.

Hold Nothing Against Each Other (Matthew 5:21–26)

21 "You have heard that it was said to those of old, 'You shall not murder, and whoever murders will be in danger of the judgment.' 22 But I say to you that whoever is angry with his brother without a cause shall be in danger of the judgment. And whoever says to his brother, 'Raca!' shall be in danger of the council. But whoever says, 'You fool!' shall be in danger of hell fire. 23 Therefore if you bring

your gift to the altar, and there remember that your brother has something against you, ^{24} leave your gift there before the altar, and go your way. First be reconciled to your brother, and then come and offer your gift. ^{25} Agree with your adversary quickly, while you are on the way with him, lest your adversary deliver you to the judge, the judge hand you over to the officer, and you be thrown into prison. ^{26} Assuredly, I say to you, you will by no means get out of there till you have paid the last penny."

---

5. Jesus begins by stating the Old Testament law regarding murder (see Exodus 20:13). But He then broadens the commands to include a person's attitudes and intentions—not just actions. He focuses on the heart issue of a need for *reconciliation*. According to Jesus, what should we consider before we approach God in worship (see Matthew 5:23)?

_____

_____

_____

_____

_____

_____

6. What priority does Jesus establish when it comes to resolving conflict and worship? What specific actions does He instruct us to take (see verses 24–26)?

_____

_____

_____

_____

_____

_____

_____

Love Your Enemies (Matthew 5:43–48)

[43] "You have heard that it was said, 'You shall love your neighbor and hate your enemy.' [44] But I say to you, love your enemies, bless those who curse you, do good to those who hate you, and pray for those who spitefully use you and persecute you, [45] that you may be sons of your Father in heaven; for He makes His sun rise on the evil and on the good, and sends rain on the just and on the unjust. [46] For if you love those who love you, what reward have you? Do not even the tax collectors do the same? [47] And if you greet your brethren only, what do you do more than others? Do not even the tax collectors do so? [48] Therefore you shall be perfect, just as your Father in heaven is perfect.

7. Jesus here states the Old Testament law regarding how God's people were to treat others (see Leviticus 19:18; Deuteronomy 23:3–6). How does Jesus expand on this command? What actions should we take when we are offended by others (see Matthew 5:43–45)?

8. What point is Jesus making about how His followers are to forgive one another? How will this serve as a witness to the world (see verses 46–47)?

_____

_____

_____

_____

_____

_____

REVIEWING THE STORY

Paul begins his short letter to Philemon with a personal greeting, a blessing, and a thanks to his friend for all the good he is doing in the church at Colossae. Paul then makes an urgent plea for Philemon to show similar concern for Onesimus, his runaway slave. Paul knows that he is negotiating from a delicate position—from a legal, cultural, and personal standpoint, Philemon's best course of action would be to deal severely with Onesimus. So Paul argues from a higher perspective. He points to Onesimus's value as a Christian brother and fellow worker.

9. How does Paul describe his relationship with Philemon (see Philemon 1:1)?

_____

_____

_____

_____

_____

_____

_____

10. Why does Paul find great joy and consolation in his friendship with Philemon (see Philemon 1:7)?

_____

_____

_____

_____

_____

_____

11. How does Paul use a play on words with Onesimus's name, which means "profitable," to help Philemon understand Onesimus's new status (see Philemon 1:10–11)?

_____

_____

_____

_____

_____

_____

12. How does Paul want Philemon to receive Onesimus (see Philemon 1:16)?

_____

_____

_____

_____

_____

_____

APPLYING THE MESSAGE

13. When is a time in your life that you felt led to intercede for someone? What happened as result?

_____

_____

_____

_____

_____

_____

_____

_____

_____

_____

14. When is a time you had to take the difficult first step to reconcile a relationship that had been strained? What happened in that situation?

_____

_____

_____

_____

_____

_____

_____

_____

_____

_____

_____

_____

REFLECTING ON THE MEANING

In the drama involving Onesimus, Paul, and Philemon, we find an extraordinary picture of God's redemptive work. Onesimus represents all sinners. Paul can be depicted in the role of the Savior. Philemon can be seen to represent Almighty God. Let's examine this more closely.

First, Onesimus represents all sinners. When Onesimus, a sinner headed for punishment, left his master and fled to the city of Rome, he headed straight toward judgment. If he had been caught, he would have been crucified, for that is how the Roman authorities treated runaway slaves. What Onesimus did in that day was illegal and immoral. He took from his owner that which did not belong to him. All of us, like Onesimus, are sinners. We have run away from God, and we have sinned in the process. Like Onesimus, we are also slaves. We are all "slaves of sin" (Romans 6:6). Until we are set free by Christ, we are rebellious runaways from God.

Second, Paul represents the Savior. Paul sends Onesimus back to his master with a message that says, "I will pay for everything that he has done." Onesimus was poor and couldn't redeem himself, so Paul knew that he had to step in to redeem him. In the same way, we each had a debt that we could not pay before we came to Christ. However, our debt was not measured in dollars, but in *death*. The almighty God sent His Son to pay the penalty for our sin. Jesus said, in effect, "I will pay for everything that they have done."

Third, Philemon represents Almighty God. According to historical sources, when Onesimus went back to Philemon, he was forgiven, released, and given his freedom. Philemon chose to release him from the debt and set him free. In the same way, when Jesus Christ paid the debt of death that we owe, God accepted that debt and gave us our freedom and our forgiveness. We have now all been set free.

So, in the story of Onesimus, Paul, and Philemon, we have an awe-inspiring illustration of the gospel in action—of Jesus making amends for us with Almighty God.

JOURNALING YOUR RESPONSE

What personal takeaways can you find in Onesimus's story? Explain.

WHAT IT MEANS TO BE A FRIEND

Philemon 1:17–25

GETTING STARTED

What is the most important quality you look for in a friend?

SETTING THE STAGE

As Paul set out to write the letter of Philemon, he understood he was testing the bonds of his friendship. After all, Onesimus not only ran away from his master but also *stole* from Philemon's household in the process. Such a matter was typically prosecuted in the courts. What Paul was asking Philemon to do instead would have likely put him at odds with his fellow slave owners. In the world of Paul's day, these slave owners would have been afraid of setting a "dangerous" precedent in forgiving and freeing a runaway slave.

Yet Paul presses Philemon on the issue for several reasons. First, he considers Philemon a "beloved friend" (Philemon 1:1). Paul was in prison and relied on support from his friends to live. He was giving Philemon an opportunity to support him. Paul also considered Philemon a fellow worker. The gospel the two men proclaimed bound them together as teammates. Paul was asking his teammate in this case to do something difficult for the sake of their team.

Paul also presses Philemon on the issue because he considers him to be a faithful brother in Christ. Paul describes his friend as a man of "love and faith" (verse 5). He was faithful in "the sharing of [his] faith" (verse 6). He was faithful in refreshing "the hearts of the saints" (verse 7). This is why Paul asks him to remember him in prayer (see verse 22).

In this final section of Paul's letter, we will see how he backs up his appeal with a personal offer to cover Onesimus's debt. He will also remind his friend of the debt that he *owes* to the apostle. In the process, he will give Philemon the opportunity to demonstrate forgiveness . . . just as God has demonstrated His forgiveness to him.

EXPLORING THE TEXT

Philemon's Obedience Encouraged (Philemon 1:17–20)

> [17] If then you count me as a partner, receive him as you would me.
> [18] But if he has wronged you or owes anything, put that on my account.

¹⁹ I, Paul, am writing with my own hand. I will repay—not to mention to you that you owe me even your own self besides. ²⁰ Yes, brother, let me have joy from you in the Lord; refresh my heart in the Lord.

---

1. Paul refers to himself as Philemon's "partner." By this, he means they are partners in the work of Christ. How does Paul appeal to Philemon's position as a fellow worker to plead for mercy for Onesimus (see verse 17)?

_____

_____

_____

_____

_____

_____

_____

_____

2. In the first century, a handwritten statement—similar to a signature in today's world—validated a document. Besides writing the letter with his own hand, how else does Paul attempt to convince Philemon to honor his request for mercy (see verses 18–20)?

_____

_____

_____

_____

_____

_____

Paul's Confidence in Philemon (Philemon 1:21–25)

21 Having confidence in your obedience, I write to you, knowing that you will do even more than I say. 22 But, meanwhile, also prepare a guest room for me, for I trust that through your prayers I shall be granted to you.

23 Epaphras, my fellow prisoner in Christ Jesus, greets you, 24 as do Mark, Aristarchus, Demas, Luke, my fellow laborers.

25 The grace of our Lord Jesus Christ be with your spirit. Amen.

3. Paul makes his case to Philemon solely by appealing to his position as a brother in Christ. What is Paul confident that Philemon will do in this regard (see verse 21)?

_____

_____

_____

_____

_____

_____

_____

_____

_____

_____

_____

_____

_____

_____

4. In asking Philemon to "prepare a guest room" for him, Paul seems hopeful that he will soon be released from prison and will be able to visit the church that meets in Philemon's home. What reason does Paul give for his hope of reuniting with Philemon and the believers in Colossae (see verse 22)?

_____

_____

_____

_____

_____

_____

_____

_____

GOING DEEPER

Paul was asking a great deal of Philemon in making his request that he forgive Onesimus. If Philemon pardoned his runaway slave, he risked losing his standing in Roman society and having similar problems with his other slaves. However, as a believer, Philemon had to recognize that he himself had received costly forgiveness. As Paul points out in the following passage, forgiveness and mercy are intended to be passed on. They are evidence of being a "new man" in Christ.

Walk Not as the World Walks (Ephesians 4:17–27)

17 This I say, therefore, and testify in the Lord, that you should no longer walk as the rest of the Gentiles walk, in the futility of their mind, 18 having their understanding darkened, being alienated from the life of God, because of the ignorance that is in them, because of the blindness of their heart; 19 who, being past feeling, have given themselves over to lewdness, to work all uncleanness with greediness.

²⁰ But you have not so learned Christ, ²¹ if indeed you have heard Him and have been taught by Him, as the truth is in Jesus: ²² that you put off, concerning your former conduct, the old man which grows corrupt according to the deceitful lusts, ²³ and be renewed in the spirit of your mind, ²⁴ and that you put on the new man which was created according to God, in true righteousness and holiness.

²⁵ Therefore, putting away lying, "Let each one of you speak truth with his neighbor," for we are members of one another. ²⁶ "Be angry, and do not sin": do not let the sun go down on your wrath, ²⁷ nor give place to the devil.

---

5. In his letter to the Ephesians, Paul is writing to believers who are being transformed daily into Christlikeness—who are no longer walking "as the rest of the Gentiles walk" (verse 17). This is not an instant transformation but a gradual process. Where does this process of renewal begin in the believer (see verses 17–24)?

6. Paul reminds the believers in Ephesus—much like he reminds Philemon—that they are all members of the same team. For this reason, what behaviors should they put away? Why was it important for them to do this (see verses 25–27)?

_____

_____

_____

_____

_____

A Transformed Life (Ephesians 4:28–32)

28 Let him who stole steal no longer, but rather let him labor, working with his hands what is good, that he may have something to give him who has need. 29 Let no corrupt word proceed out of your mouth, but what is good for necessary edification, that it may impart grace to the hearers. 30 And do not grieve the Holy Spirit of God, by whom you were sealed for the day of redemption. 31 Let all bitterness, wrath, anger, clamor, and evil speaking be put away from you, with all malice. 32 And be kind to one another, tenderhearted, forgiving one another, even as God in Christ forgave you.

7. Paul recognized that a transformation had occurred in Onesimus's life after he had become a follower of Christ. In his letter to the Ephesians, what are some of the traits that Paul says will accompany a life this is truly transformed by the gospel (see verses 28–29)?

_____

_____

_____

_____

_____

8. Paul stresses that followers of Christ should not be wrapped up in thoughts of vengeance but should seek to extend forgiveness and reconciliation in their relationships. Why is it critical for believers to put aside such feelings of wrath and bitterness (see verses 30–32)?

_____

_____

_____

_____

_____

_____

REVIEWING THE STORY

Paul concludes his letter with a heartfelt appeal to Philemon as a friend, partner, brother in Christ, and recipient of God's forgiveness. He offers to assume any debt that Onesimus owes Philemon. He then reminds Philemon of the debt that he owes Paul—since Paul was the one who led him to Christ. Paul gives Philemon an opportunity to minister to him and bring joy to his life by offering Onesimus compassion and grace. Paul expresses his confidence that Philemon will surpass his expectations in doing the right thing. He closes with a few words about staying with Philemon after he is released from imprisonment.

9. What offer does Paul make regarding the things Onesimus may have stolen from Philemon when he ran away (see Philemon 1:18)?

_____

_____

_____

_____

_____

10. What reminder does Paul offer Philemon on the subject of debts that were owed to people (see Philemon 1:19)?

11. What distinction does Paul make between Epaphras and the other friends he mentions at the end of his letter (see Philemon 1:23–24)?

12. What final benediction does the apostle Paul offer to his friend (see Philemon 1:25)?

APPLYING THE MESSAGE

13. What is the biggest challenge you face when it comes to your friendships?

_____

_____

_____

_____

_____

_____

_____

_____

_____

_____

_____

14. How are you currently following the example of Jesus as a friend to your brothers and sisters in Christ?

_____

_____

_____

_____

_____

_____

_____

_____

_____

_____

_____

REFLECTING ON THE MEANING

Paul's letter to Philemon shows us that God brings people into our lives for a *reason*. Against the backdrop of slavery, the lives of three men intersected, and all three men were affected in a profound way. Philemon and Onesimus both encountered Paul, who introduced them to Christ. They became, spiritually speaking, "new men." For his part, Paul found joy in his relationships with Philemon and Onesimus. It was the joy a father might feel in seeing his children thrive. Paul reveled in seeing the Lord's transformational work in their lives.

The New Testament narrative ends before Onesimus returns to Philemon. But as we have mentioned, there is historical evidence that suggests Onesimus was changed by the experience. We find this evidence in the works of a man named Ignatius, who some fifty years after the encounter was being transported to Rome for execution. In one letter, written to the believers in Ephesus, Ignatius has much good to say about their bishop—a man named *Onesimus*. Ignatius even makes the same pun on Onesimus's name that Paul made in his letter of Philemon. He talks about Onesimus being "profitable to Christ."

Based on this evidence, we can conclude that Philemon likely *did* show the escaped slave some measure of grace and forgiveness when Onesimus returned to the city of Colossae bearing the apostle Paul's letter. Philemon, without realizing it, may have played a role in God's plan to promote Onesimus from an escaped slave to the bishop of Ephesus! Philemon was certainly also changed by the episode. He grew in Christlikeness by demonstrating grace and forgiveness. He even may have been able to rejoice in Onesimus's ministry in Ephesus and the role that God allowed him to play in it.

With this story in mind, let us consider our own potential for impacting other people's lives by being quick to show grace, mercy, and forgiveness. We have no way of knowing what God has in store for us or for the people who cross our paths. What we do know is that God can do something powerful at those intersections.

JOURNALING YOUR RESPONSE

When has a friend helped you see your need to forgive someone?

LEADER'S GUIDE

Thank you for choosing to lead your group through this study from Dr. David Jeremiah on *The Letters of Colossians & Philemon*. Being a group leader has its own rewards, and it is our prayer that your walk with the Lord will deepen through this experience. During the twelve lessons in this study, you and your group will read selected passages from these letters, explore key themes in them based on teachings from Dr. Jeremiah, and review questions that will encourage group discussion. There are multiple components in this section that can help you structure your lessons and discussion time, so please be sure to read and consider each one.

BEFORE YOU BEGIN

Before your first meeting, make sure you and your group are well-versed with the content of the lesson. Group members should have their own copy of *The Letters of Colossians & Philemon study guide* this study guide prior to the first meeting so they can follow along and record their answers, thoughts, and insights. After the first week, you may wish to assign the study guide lesson as homework prior to the group meeting and then use the meeting time to discuss the content in the lesson.

To ensure everyone has a chance to participate in the discussion, the ideal size for a group is around eight to ten people. If there are more than ten people, break up the bigger group into smaller subgroups. Make sure the members are committed to participating each week, as this will help create stability and help you better prepare the structure of the meeting.

At the beginning of each week's study, start with the opening Getting Started question to introduce the topic you will be discussing. The members should answer briefly, as the goal is just for them to have an idea of the subject in their minds as you go over the lesson. This will allow the members to become engaged and ready to interact with the rest of the group.

After reviewing the lesson, try to initiate a free-flowing discussion. Invite group members to bring questions and insights they may have discovered to the next meeting, especially if they were unsure of the meaning of some parts of the lesson. Be prepared to discuss how biblical truth applies to the world we live in today.

WEEKLY PREPARATION

As the group leader, here are a few things that you can do to prepare for each meeting:

- *Be thoroughly familiar with the material in the lesson.* Make sure that you understand the content of each lesson so you know how to structure the group time and are prepared to lead the group discussion.

- *Decide, ahead of time, which questions you want to discuss.* Depending on how much time you have each week, you may not be able to reflect on every question. Select specific questions that you feel will evoke the best discussion.

- *Take prayer requests.* At the end of your discussion, take prayer requests from your group members and then pray for one another.

STRUCTURING THE DISCUSSION TIME

There are several ways to structure the duration of the study. You can choose to cover each lesson individually, for a total of twelve weeks of group meetings, or you can combine two lessons together per week, for a total of six weeks of group meetings. The following charts illustrate these options: